In the Beginning

IN THE BEGINNING

A JOURNEY THROUGH GENESIS

by Jack Finegan

HARPER & BROTHERS, PUBLISHERS, NEW YORK

Grateful acknowledgment is made to the following for permission to quote from the works indicated:

Abingdon Press, Nashville: *The Interpreter's Bible*, Volume I, copyright 1952 by Pierce and Smith.

Channel Press, Great Neck: *The Cup of Fury* by Upton Sinclair, copyright © 1956 by Upton Sinclair.

Farrar, Straus & Cudahy, Inc., New York: *Rivers in the Desert* by Nelson Glueck, copyright © 1959 by Nelson Glueck.

The University of Chicago Press, Chicago: *Systematic Theology*, Volume I, by Paul Tillich, copyright 1951 by The University of Chicago Press.

The Westminster Press, Philadelphia: *A History of Israel* by John Bright, copyright © 1959 by W. L. Jenkins.

Library of Congress catalog card number: 62-7286

CONTENTS

Preface   7

1. Creation (Genesis 1:1-2:3)   9

2. Paradise Lost (Genesis 2:4-3:24)   19

3. East of Eden, or Murder Inaugurated (Genesis 4)   27

4. The Flood (Genesis 5:1-9:17)   39

5. Noah and His Wine (Genesis 9:18-29)   51

6. The Family of Man (Genesis 10)   64

7. The Tower of Babel (Genesis 11:1-9)   74

8. Abraham: Man of Faith (Genesis 11:10-17:27)   85

9. Sodom and Gomorrah: Can It Happen Now?
      (Genesis 18-19)   100

10. The Sacrifice (Almost) of Isaac (Genesis 20-23)   112

11. Climbing Jacob's Ladder with Him (Genesis 24-36)   122

12. The Providence of God in Joseph's Life and Ours
      (Genesis 37-50)   131

Notes   143

Scripture Index   151

Name and Subject Index   158

PREFACE

This volume begins a journey through the Bible. As with every journey, one does not know how long it will take or, indeed, if it will ever be possible to finish it. Every journey is subject to unforeseen interruption or even termination. But to start on any journey means at least to start with a sense of direction, and that is good. For a long time I have endeavored to consider the discoveries of archeology in the Bible lands throughout the whole period within which the Old Testament and the New Testament belong. Now I venture to express my opinions (even on many highly debatable problems and ones where presently prevailing opinion is much different, yet where there are not lacking signs in our time that others are moving too in directions toward which I try to point) on the relation of recorded biblical events to what is known, archeologically, of the background from which the Bible is supposed to have come. I shall attempt to show that the Bible fits into that background very well; in fact, so very well that the biblical records cannot, on the whole, be "cleverly devised myths" (II Peter 1:16) but are, rather, substantially dependable reports of actual happenings in which real people participated and in which they believed God was dealing with them. Since those happenings often concerned their faith, our faith too, which stands in a line of connection with theirs, cannot ignore these reports. Beginning at the beginning, we shall try to see what the Bible tells, and what that which it tells means to us.

JACK FINEGAN

7

1 CREATION (*Genesis 1:1-2:3*)

The natural starting point for a journey through the Bible is the first chapter of the first book, namely, Genesis, Chapter 1 (or, more exactly, Chapter 1 plus its proper continuation which our chapter and verse division marks as the first three verses of Chapter 2). This section describes the creation, and that event, as such, is also the necessary point from which to start along the way that is unfolded in the Bible.

What kind of account is this, that is given of the creation in Genesis 1? Is it a scientific account? Science assumes that a process of events is going on, and inquires into the relation between things in space and time. Then we must expect a truly scientific account to be literally accurate as to the external facts it reports. This, Genesis 1 is not. When that fact was first discovered it caused glee for the skeptics who took delight in pointing out the inconsistencies in the narrative, and it occasioned pain for the believers who tried to defend the record in its literal details against the theories of Copernicus, Darwin, and their successors. That creation took place in seven successive days of twenty-four hours each, which is what the narrative says if we must take it literally, and that this was in the year 4004 B.C., which was the date arrived at by one famous authority as he added up the several chronological notations throughout the Bible, is obviously not to be squared with the currently prevailing views in science as to how the world came into being. But instead of leading us to dismiss Genesis 1 from any serious consideration, this may simply point us to the fact that this account is not even intended primarily to be of a scientific character.

Is it a philosophical account? Philosophy assumes all the various states of affairs in the universe, and asks after underlying principles. If Genesis 1 is primarily of philosophical significance then we should have to look at it as essentially a symbol of timeless truths. Paul Tillich is a philosophical theologian, and he seems to put the matter entirely in this light when he says: "The doctrine of creation is not the story of an event which took place 'once upon a time.' It is the basic description of the relation between God and the world."[1] Much as this statement contains an element of truth, recognition of which will be found again below, it seems to the present writer that the Genesis account of creation describes something that "happened," an event or events after which things were not as they were before, and accordingly the account cannot be considered as purely philosophical.

Is it, then, a theological account? There is assuredly a place for what has been called the "serene curiosity" of science and of philosophy, and for the kind of questions which these disciplines raise, but there is also an unavoidable place for the raising of a different kind of question. We are not only spectators but also participants in life. Since our life is precarious and dependent, we are almost inevitably driven, at least sometimes, to deep concern about it. At best there is mystery about our life, at worst there is tragedy in it. We are constrained, at least sometimes, to ask: Who or what has put me here? What forces determine my life? What does my life mean and where is it going?

These are commonly recognized to be "religious" questions. They are interrogations about the ultimate ground and meaning of our existence. They are queries about the ultimate origin of everything. Whence comes our life? Upon what does it depend?

It is to questions such as these that Genesis 1 gives a theological answer. There was science in the ancient world, for both the Babylonians and the Egyptians made important advances in such fields as mathematics, astronomy, geology, chemistry, and medicine. There was philosophy in the ancient world, for the Greek thinkers left all succeeding Western philosophers in their debt. But the Israelites, from whom the book of Genesis and the other Old Testament books come, were not primarily scientific or speculative in their concerns. They were, however, deeply concerned with the mystery of existence, with the purpose and meaning of their history as a people, and with the meaning and purpose of the life of man. We can say only that as they pondered these questions an illumination came to them which can also become meaningful to us as we consider the same questions. It provides an answer which we cannot so much prove or demonstrate, as we attempt to do with regard to matters of science and philosophy, but which we can affirm and trust. The answer is essentially that we are creatures of God, that we are dependent upon him, that he has made all things, that his power and love are sovereign in all things. Since this is an answer which refers to God, it is properly called a theological answer.

In the first chapter of Genesis this answer is given in the form of a story or a poem about God. The sophisticated theologian likes to call this a myth, a term which we may prefer to avoid since it has so many possible meanings. What is meant, at all events, is a form of expression which understands and states in the language of human action that which transcends man. Thus we are told that at one time God did such and such things. Now we realize upon reflection that limited human understanding can-

not possibly comprehend the when and the what and the how
of the full action of God. So we have to say that the story in
Genesis 1 tells about an event or events in our language, but at
the same time points to something which goes beyond our full
knowing. Indeed, is it not the very genius of poetry to do this
very thing? Therefore, it may be that the word "poem" is the
best of all to apply to the account with which we are dealing.
At any rate, we may say concerning the account of creation what
Langdon Gilkey says in his book *Maker of Heaven and Earth,*
a work which states much more fully the matters with which our
present chapter is dealing: "It is a true, although not literal,
affirmation about the relation of the whole system of facts in the
world to their Creator God."[2]

What does this account tell us? It tells us that there was a
beginning. It opens with the words: "In the beginning." It is
not possible to think of God as having a beginning, or an ending.
If God had a beginning or an ending, he would be a limited
being like ourselves. Therefore, we speak of him as eternal. "From
everlasting to everlasting thou art God."[3] But we do speak about
a beginning of the universe. Genesis 1:1 states that "in the beginning God created the heavens and the earth." This must mean,
it seems, that God then created time itself. If time were already
going on, then there was a time that was before the beginning.
This is to raise the child's familiar question, What was before
the beginning? Therefore, the interpretation is suggested that at
that point God created time itself. This at any rate was the conclusion of Augustine as he pondered the matter. He said: "For,
though Himself eternal, and without beginning, yet He caused
time to have a beginning; and man, whom He had not previously
made He made in time. . . . God, without change of will, created
man, who had never before been, and gave him an existence in
time."[4] There was a beginning.

Next, the account points us to the probable fact that there was

a creation of everything out of nothing. Genesis 1:2 might appear
to indicate that chaos already existed, and God simply went to
work upon it in order to accomplish creation: "The earth was
without form and void, and darkness was upon the face of the
deep; and the Spirit of God was moving over the face of the
waters." But the preceding verse seems to make it plain that at
"the beginning" there was only God; therefore, in creation God
must first have made the formless deep, and then have brought
it into order. This interpretation is strengthened when the implications of the chief alternative possibilities are considered. One
alternative to our conclusion has already been noted, namely,
the idea that God created everything out of something. This is
the view of dualism, which supposes that there was already
something there besides God. In the mythologies of many ancient
religions, creation is accomplished when God wrestles with and
subdues some monster of chaos. In our own experience, we know
that whenever man makes something he always makes it out of
something, out of wood, or stone, or clay, or another material.
But to transfer this analogy to God results in a limited view of
God. God is limited, because over against him is self-existent
stuff. He is not really creator, but only manufacturer. A dis-
paraging view of matter is usually also the result of the adoption
of this conception. Since God, on the one hand, must be thought
of as good, the material with which he works, on the other hand,
is usually considered to be lacking in goodness and even to be
evil. Accordingly, Irenaeus long ago repudiated the transfer to
God of the human analogy of making something out of something: "While men, indeed, cannot make anything out of nothing,
but only out of matter already existing, yet God is in this point
pre-eminently superior to men, that He Himself called into being
the substance of His creation, when previously it had no
existence."[5]

Another alternative is the supposition that God created everything out of himself. This answer corresponds to the position of monism or pantheism. It may seem attractive, for it would enable us to say that God is in everything. But if God is only the sum total of everything, then again he is limited. And if finite things and persons are of value only because they are small portions of God, then they are not of value in themselves. In practice, pantheism usually leads to a desire to escape from an existence fettered by space and time, and to return to more immediate union with God. Therefore, this position also does not correspond with the biblical understanding of the nature of God and the nature of his created world. Irenaeus, again, expressed the repudiation of this view:

But the things established are distinct from Him who has established them, and what have been made from Him who has made them. For He is Himself uncreated, both without beginning and end, . . . but the things which have been made by Him have received a beginning. But whatever things had a beginning, and are liable to dissolution, and are subject to and stand in need of Him who made them, must necessarily in all respects have a different term [applied to them].[6]

Since, therefore, the alternative views of dualism and of monism contain difficulties which are apparently insuperable, we are driven back to what is probably the main line of Christian interpretation. It will not do to say that God made the world out of something that was already there, nor that he made it out of himself; therefore, we must say that he made everything out of nothing. He is not like ourselves just an artificer or organizer, but is in the profound biblical sense of the word the creator, the one who called into being the things which were not in being.

Yet again, Genesis 1 tells us that there was a creation in progressive steps. The framework of the chapter consists of a week of days. In six days of active work, God made the universe, on the seventh day he rested. The sequence is actually not too far different from that which we might construct upon the basis of modern science. On the first day God made light. Light, which is energy in luminous form, is perhaps the most wonderful thing in the world. It is no accident that in many of the ancient religions, the chief gods were gods of light, such as Re and Aten in Egypt, and Ahura Mazda in Persia. In Israel, light was of course not itself deified, but it was that which, according to Genesis 1, God made on the very first day of creation. On the second day he made the firmament, the splendid expanse over our heads. On the third day he made the good earth, bearing all manner of plants. On the fourth day he made the sun and moon and stars. On the fifth day he caused the waters to bring forth swarms of living creatures, a conception quite in line with modern ideas as to where life took its origin, and he made birds to fly above the earth. On the sixth day he called the animals into being and he made man, this close connection of man with the animals also having a similarity to modern theories on the same subject. Such were the steps in God's creative work on six successive days, after which, on the seventh day, he rested. Since the author of the account wrote, as we have maintained, in a poetic way, he may himself have intended by his "days" not necessarily literal days of twenty-four hours each but, rather, great successive periods of God's creative activity.

Once more, this account tells us that creation is good. The repeated refrain which recurs throughout the chapter is: "And God saw that it was good." Dualism usually makes the creation evil; monism usually makes it unreal and illusory. In both cases the world is to be looked down upon, and to be gotten out of as soon as possible. Not so, according to the first chapter of Genesis. According to this account the creation is good.

What, then, does this account do for us? It gives us a line of movement to go along. Because there is a beginning there is a line running on from that beginning into the future. Time, if the interpretation advanced above is correct, has its beginning, and from there is goes on toward where it has never been before. This conception may not seem so remarkable to us as it doubtless would have seemed if we had lived in the ancient world. There the prevailing view was that time is a cyclical movement, and that everything goes around through ceaseless circles. So the Greeks and Romans believed; so too did the Hindus and Jains. According to the Israelite doctrine, however, time runs on from its beginning point into a future that is always new and different. Since this movement is a part of God's arrangement of the world it must be guided by him. Time is not our enemy, much as some of us think it is and would seek to resist it if we could. It moves toward some culmination, the ultimate intent of which cannot be outside the purpose of God.

The teaching set forth in the first chapter of Genesis also gives us an intelligible world to live in. The vast forces amidst which our lives are set, are not chaotic. The Spirit of God moved upon the deep and brought things into orderly arrangement. Although the interplay of the great forces of the universe sometimes appears inimical to us and sometimes even results in disaster for us, the whole is neither a chaos nor a diabolical contrivance. It is susceptible to understanding, it is an order of events which does have a meaning and does move toward a goal, dimly discerned though the meaning and the goal may be at any particular moment.

Likewise, Genesis 1 gives us a good world to work with and rejoice in. The creation is good, and life in it is fundamentally good. In that case we ought always to look for the goodness that is in the created world in which we are. In the biography of Alice Freeman Palmer, written by her husband Professor George Herbert Palmer, there is a story of the club she conducted for small girls in a tenement area of Boston. This was called "The Happiness Club," and one of the club rules was that each girl

must see something beautiful every day. In the shabby houses
and dreary streets where these girls lived, that rule was not easy
to follow. But with the eagerness of little children, they undertook
to live up to it. One saw a sparrow splashing in a rain gutter,
another noticed the way the sunshine fell on the baby's hair.[7]
It is possible to live in far more beautiful parts of the world, but
to be too preoccupied or morose to see the beauty. But since ours
is a good creation, it behooves us to look for that goodness everywhere.

Finally, the biblical account of creation gives us a great God
to worship and praise. We have said that that account is the result of an illumination which came to the Israelites as they pondered the ultimate questions of life. That means that we consider
it a revelation which was vouchsafed to them, a revelation of
which we can be the beneficiaries too, as we also, in similar concern, accept it and affirm it. So accepted and affirmed, the knowledge of the Creator delivers us from despair about the world,
as we have seen, and guards us from idolatry toward the world.
No created thing or person can be the proper object of worship
by us. Only God the Creator, the great God who made all things,
may we rightly worship and praise. Irenaeus stated the conclusion
of the matter in Christian terms when he wrote: "He indeed who
made all things can alone, together with His Word, properly be
termed God and Lord: but the things which have been made
cannot have this term applied to them, neither should they justly
assume that appellation which belongs to the Creator."[8] It is
strictly in line with this thought, and with the basic doctrine of
creation in Genesis, Chapter 1, that in the 19th Psalm and in
Joseph Addison's stately paraphrase of the same, all created
things are heard to praise their Creator:

> The spacious firmament on high,
> With all the blue ethereal sky,
> And spangled heav'ns, a shining frame,

Their great Original proclaim:
The unwearied sun, from day to day,
Does his Creator's power display,
And publishes to every land
The work of an Almighty hand.

Soon as the evening shades prevail,
The moon takes up the wondrous tale,
And nightly to the listening earth,
Repeats the story of her birth;
While all the stars that round her burn,
And all the planets in their turn,
Confirm the tidings as they roll,
And spread the truth from pole to pole.

What tho' in solemn silence all
Move round the dark terrestrial ball?
What tho' no real voice nor sound
Amid the radiant orbs be found?
In reason's ear they all rejoice,
And utter forth a glorified voice;
Forever singing, as they shine,
"The hand that made us is divine."[9]

2 PARADISE LOST (Genesis 2:4-3:24)

If the first chapter of Genesis is a majestic poem about the creative work of God, the second and third chapters contain a vivid story about man. In these chapters we meet Adam and, accordingly, our first question must be, Who was Adam? The Hebrew word *'adam* is originally a common noun, meaning "man." Like the corresponding word in English, it can mean either a human being, thus "a man," or "the man," or all human beings together, that is, "man" in the sense of "mankind." In Assyrian, which is also a Semitic language, *adāmu* means "made" or "produced"; according to this possible etymology, man as *'adam* is a being who was made or produced, that is, a creature. In Hebrew, the feminine form of the word, *'adamah,* means "ground"; thus the very name reminds us that man was made, as Genesis 2:7 states, of dust from the ground. Man, therefore, is a creature made out of the common elements of the universe.

At the same time, however, the Hebrew word *adam* can be a proper noun, that is to say, a name. The problem is, therefore, where to translate the word in the one way, and where in the other way. Actually in the translation of Genesis almost everyone agrees to begin with the general sense of the word, and the term

is rendered as "man" in Genesis 2:7 in all the major versions including the King James, the Revised Standard, and Moffatt. Thus
the King James Version: "The Lord God formed man of the dust
of the ground." At Genesis 2:19, where the animals are brought
to be named, the King James Version begins to use the proper
name "Adam," but the Revised Standard Version says correctly,
because the Hebrew still has the article, that he "brought them
to the man." At Genesis 3:17, where one cannot tell whether the
Hebrew has the article or not, the Revised Standard Version begins to use the proper name, but Moffatt continues, probably
more correctly,[1] to render: "To the man he [the Lord God] said."
Only at Genesis 4:25 and 5:1 is the word plainly used without
the article, and Moffatt, the Revised Standard Version, and the
King James Version all give the personal name, Adam. Thus
Moffatt, in 5:1: "Here is the list of Adam's descendants."

The narrative in Chapters 2 and 3 of Genesis is, therefore, a
story about "man." "Man" may be individualized and personalized
so that we might almost speak of him, as we would in modern
parlance, as "Mr. Adam"; he is at the same time all mankind and,
accordingly, there is a sense in which he includes ourselves.

It is next stated, in Genesis 2:8, that the Lord God put the man
in a garden which he planted in Eden, and our next question, accordingly, is, Where was Eden? The verse says that the place was
"eastward" (kjv), or "in the east" (rsv). If the account was
written from the viewpoint of Palestine, this would suggest a location to the east of Palestine. As for the name Eden, in Sumerian
and Babylonian *edinu* means "plain" and was applied to the flat
land of Lower Mesopotamia. The account also mentions a river
which flowed out of Eden, and divided and became four rivers
named the Pishon, Gihon, Hiddekel, and Euphrates. The
Euphrates we know, for it still has the same name. Of the
Hiddekel the Hebrew says literally that it flows "in front of"
Assyria. This is usually translated to mean "east of," but from

the viewpoint of Palestine a river that flowed in front of Assyria would be "west of" Assyria, and Moffatt is probably correct in giving the latter translation. The Hiddekel, then, must have been the Tigris. Since the Tigris and Euphrates are the two great rivers of Mesopotamia, we have confirmation thus far for centering Eden in the Mesopotamian region. The two remaining rivers are also identified by some with canals in Mesopotamia and, if that were correct, we could localize Eden completely within that area. The Gihon, however, is said to flow around the whole land of Cush. Cush was on the Upper Nile and, in Old Testament usage, included Ethiopia, these being regions from which conquerors and rulers of Egypt not infrequently came. Therefore, the Gihon was probably the Nile. The Ethiopians called it the Gēyōn, and Josephus made this identification. The Pishon, likewise, is said to flow around the whole land of Havilah, a land of gold, bdellium, and onyx. In Genesis 10:7 Havilah is mentioned along with Seba and Sheba, which were the names of kingdoms in South Arabia; in Genesis 10:29 it is included with Ophir, too, and there is recent evidence that Ophir may have been in India. Arabia and India were both famous for gold; bdellium is something with which the manna was compared in Numbers 11:7, and therefore it was probably the aromatic gum which Pliny tells about in his *Natural History* and which came from Arabia and India; the onyx stone also is mentioned by Pliny as coming specially from India and Arabia. It is difficult to find a great river in Arabia, but in India there were the Indus and the Ganges. Josephus thought the Pishon was the Ganges; since the Indus is nearer to the other rivers and was, in fact, famous in very early times, it seems likely that we should identify the Pishon with the Indus. The demarcation of Eden is made, accordingly, on a large scale. It is the four great rivers of the ancient world that are mentioned, the Tigris and Euphrates, the Nile and Indus. In other words, what we are told is that the Lord God planted a garden in the Middle East and, in fact, the Middle East, specially along the valleys of its four great rivers, was a garden land in ancient times.

In Hebrew and in Greek there was another word for a watered garden, or a park of pleasure. This word is directly transliterated into English as "paradise," and it is this word which is used in the Greek translation of Genesis 2:8: "And the Lord God planted a paradise in Eden toward the rising [of the sun]." This, then, is where the Lord God placed the man whom he made, in a garden in Eden, in paradise.

Although we have now traced as well as we can the geographical allusions in the account in order to ascertain the author's conception, since we have called this a story about man, we can well agree with the comment of someone who says that "Eden belongs less in the realm of geography than in the soul of man."[2] From this point of view we may say further, in answer to the question with which we are presently dealing, that Eden was where we were before things went wrong. When the first astronaut stood upon the surface of the moon he was allowed, in the imagination of Carlton C. Allen,[3] just one hour free from his multitudinous duties of observation and report. With his mind at rest, and standing amidst a silent desolation, it suddenly seemed as if a voice were reminding him that he was upon a thus far uncontaminated heavenly body. Here no lie had ever yet been told, here no blood spilled. This was a sample of the universe as the Creator made it, this was the purity of the world when God first gave it to man. Then the sphere of earth rose upon the horizon, and the gaze of the astronaut swept in a moment from pole to pole and over continents and oceans. All was shining bright. From this distance no stain appeared, and the earth looked as pure as the moon upon which he stood. But the astronaut knew that this was not so. He loved his earth home, but he knew that men had filled it with hatred, greed, and violence. So he found himself praying the prayer of the ancient prophet who spoke of being a

man of unclean lips and dwelling in a world of people with unclean lips. That is the wistfulness with which we look back
toward Eden. Eden is where we all were before things went
wrong.

What was the fall? The fall was something which happened.
Among all the trees in that beautiful paradise, we are told by the
account in Genesis, there were two special ones, the tree of life,
and the tree of the knowledge of good and evil. Of the latter tree
the Lord God told the man not to eat. But one of the wild
creatures, the serpent, suggested to the woman who was now the
companion of the man that there would not really be any dire
consequences if they did eat, and that it would really be desirable
to know good and evil because then they would be like God. So
the woman ate some of the fruit, and gave some to her husband
and he ate. Then they suddenly were ashamed of themselves, and
they hid when they heard God coming.

The fact that this is a story means that we do not have to take
it literally, but the fact that it is a story of an event means that we
must reckon seriously with the fact that the fall is something that
happened. In the beginning God created everything, and saw that
everything was good. After that, this event took place. The structure of creation is good; it is in what has taken place since, that
there is evil. Since this is a story about man we know that it has
to do with us, but since it is a story about an event we learn that
evil is something which takes place, not something which is necessarily so.

The theologian expresses the point we are making by using
philosophical terms. Evil, he says, is not ontological, a necessary
part of being; evil is, rather, historical, something that is not
necessary, but that is actual. If we held dualistically that God
made everything out of something, then we might consider, as the
ancient Greeks and Gnostics did, that this "something" was vile
matter, and that we will have to suffer evil as long as we have to

struggle against matter. If we held monistically that God created everything out of himself, then we might consider, as the Asian religions generally have done, that evil arises out of our ignorance, swathed as we are in a veil of illusion and thus kept apart from him to whom we truly belong. Or if we held naturalistically that God might be left out of account altogether, and that everything is the result of the blind working of natural forces, then we might consider, as the secular modern view usually does, that evil arises when the vast but blind and purposeless forces to which we are exposed in this universe happen to affect us negatively. But the first chapter of Genesis has already guarded us against these inadequate conceptions of creation, and the present account is our guard against the conclusions to which they lead, which assign a place to evil in the very structure of things. No, this account teaches, it is in history that evil has come into the world which God made as a good world. The fall is something which has taken place, and which takes place, for as Emil Brunner says: "Every man is his own Adam."

What was the result of the fall? The result of the fall was that man confronted evils which were too much for him to manage. In the garden of Eden he already had to work, for, according to Genesis 2:15, God put him there to till the garden and keep it. But when he was cast out, it seemed as if the ground were cursed; his toil and sweat were often enough rewarded with thorns and thistles. In the garden, already, man was subject to death, for he had not yet put forth his hand to take of the tree of life (Genesis 3:22). To be of dust and to return to the dust (Genesis 3:19) was his natural state and, in unbroken fellowship with God, there was nothing terrible about this. Now, however, when the fellowship was destroyed and man was cast out of the garden, death itself loomed up as a great terror. Death, which in and of itself could be natural and unfearful, must for the guilty sinner inevitably be tinged with dread. As Cuthbert A. Simpson says, for the author of this account "not death itself but man's attitude toward death as the final frustration of a frustrated life was the last consequence of the alienation from God which his rebellion had caused."[4]

As far as we can see, even in a good creation each thing must have its own nature and follow its own pattern. Only so is there an intelligible order. But as the weather follows its patterns, it may form a tornado; as the rocks follow theirs, they may produce an earthquake; as the cells follow theirs, under certain conditions a cancer may grow. Yet all such things are at least subject to investigation, to planning, and to the taking of countermeasures. To that extent they are not completely beyond our managing. But it is the evils which have come into the world through human wrong choices that build up to such demonic proportions they seem beyond our ability to cope with, as when a drift toward war is universally dreaded but cannot be halted. Since these evils arise within the area of human choices, the very discovery that wrong choices have been made is the revelation of something which one has obviously found it impossible to manage. The result of the fall is that fallen man is up against evil that is too much for him.

What can we do about it? We cannot go back to Eden. This is true of all the past, and it is especially true of obtaining the knowledge of good and evil. One can never again return to the state of prior innocence. A wrong once done, one can never again go back to the time and condition before it was committed. When man was cast out of the garden, the cherubim and a flaming sword which turned every way were set to guard the gateway so that he could not come back.

But the implications of the Genesis account are not without hope. Given a positioning of evil in the structure of things, as in the dualistic, monistic, and naturalistic views noted above, there is indeed reason for pessimism, and pessimism is usually the result of these philosophies. Evil is seen as a necessary part of being. Given, however, the view of Genesis that the creation is good and that evil comes from wrong human choice, then evil although actual is not necessary, and the freedom that is exercised in turning away from God may also be exercised in turning unto him. Thus at last it is not the innocence of Eden to which we can hope to return, but the kingdom of the God who receives repentant sinners into which we may hope to be received.

In the imaginary story referred to above, we left the astronaut praying a prayer for forgiveness. This is what everyone must do, who looks back wistfully to the Eden where we all once were. Thereupon it seemed as if God spoke to the astronaut and told him that he still loved his creation and believed in it. And so it was that when the astronaut spoke into his microphone the message from the moon for which multitudes were waiting upon earth, he spoke simply the words of the Lord's Prayer: ". . . lead us away from temptation and deliver us from evil. For thine is the everlasting kingdom. . . ."

3 EAST OF EDEN, OR MURDER INAUGURATED (*Genesis 4*)

To Adam and Eve a son was born. The marvel of his birth seemed so wonderful that when the mother saw the little baby, she cried out: "I have gotten a man with the help of the Lord."[1] In Hebrew the word "get" is *qanah*. So they gave the baby a name which sounded like the word, and called him Cain.

Another son was born, and they called him Abel. No explanation of this name is given. We know, however, that in Hebrew this word means "breath." This sugggests something transitory and evanescent. "Every man is a mere breath."[2] One wonders if there was an unconscious premonition of the brevity of life which this child would have.

The two boys grew up together, but they chose different kinds of work, and they became different kinds of persons. One day they had a grievous argument, and Cain struck Abel and killed him. Thus murder was inaugurated in the world, according to the record of Genesis 4.

What were the reasons for that murder? One reason was rivalry. In the study of anthropology, we surmise that man originally had to gather wild grains, berries, and fruits, and chase wild animals, in order to obtain food. Gradually he learned to plant seeds, cultivate fields, and grow crops. Also he tamed some of the animals, kept them closer to himself, and had flocks and herds. In the present account Cain and Abel represent the originators of these two occupations. Cain was a farmer who tilled the soil. Abel was a shepherd who kept the flocks. There in the Near East until today these are the two major occupations. There on the fertile lands, arable and irrigable, are the growers of crops. There on the pasture lands, rolling and rocky, are the watchers of flocks. There and almost everywhere there has been rivalry between these two. Sheep crop the grass so close to the soil that nothing can grow for a long time after they pass. Farmers put up barricades for protection, and the free grazing lands begin to disappear. So it was in our own West when cattlemen and sheepherders and farmers quarreled and fought. So, too, it evidently was at this early time when Cain became a farmer and Abel a shepherd.

Resentment was another factor. Cain may have already had resentment against God. Both he and Abel, it is narrated, made offerings to God. Each seemed to make an appropriate offering. Cain, out of his agricultural life, brought fruit from the ground. Abel, out of his pastoral life, brought firstlings from the flock. Since each offering seems appropriate to the one who made it, the story must be hinting that there was some crucial difference in the attitude of the two men, for the Lord approved of Abel and what he brought but not of Cain and what he brought. Hebrews 11:4, at any rate, says that this is exactly what happened: "By faith Abel offered to God a more acceptable sacrifice than Cain." Why might Cain already have had a resentment against God which spoiled the character of his offering? Was it because of his hard lot? Presumably they still lived just outside the gate of paradise. Inside were all manner of pleasant trees and good fruits. Outside, here, it was the way the Lord had told Adam it would be. The ground brought forth thorns and thistles more readily than good crops. Cain knew how to tell the weeds from the good plants. If he pulled up everything, what came up again were the weeds. In toil he was eating of the ground all the days of his life. God had put Adam and Eve out of the garden. Perhaps that was right, although it might seem as if God himself were to blame for having arranged things the way he did in the first place. But God was now keeping him, Cain, out too, and Cain surely was not to blame for what had happened before he even came on the scene. So he often looked toward the cherubim and the flaming sword which barred the gate of paradise, and he felt bitter toward God for causing him to endure this hard life. He would make an offering if he had to, because it was expected of him, but his heart was not in it. Such a reconstruction of the psychological situation is given by Byron in his poem "Cain" and it is a fact that a poet is often the best interpreter of what was originally a poetic narrative. Thus Byron's Cain ponders alone:

> And this is
> Life! Toil! and wherefore should I tell?—because
> My father could not keep his place in Eden.
> What had *I* done in this?—I was unborn,
> I sought not to be born; nor love the state
> To which that birth has brought me. Why did he
> Yield to the serpent and the woman? or,
> Yielding, why suffer? What was there in this?
> The tree was planted, and why not for him?
> If not, why place him near it, where it grew,
> The fairest in the centre? They have but
> One answer to all questions, "'twas *his* will,
> and *he* is good." How know I that? Because
> He is all-powerful, must all-good, too, follow?
> I judge but by the fruits—and they are bitter—
> Which I must feed on for a fault not mine.
> Whom have we here?—a shape like to the angels,
> Yet of a sterner and a sadder aspect,
> Of spiritual essence: why do I quake?
> Why should I fear him more than other spirits,

Whom I see daily wave their fiery swords
Before the gates round which I linger oft,
In twilight's hour, to catch a glimpse of those
Gardens which are my just inheritance,
Ere the night closes o'er the inhibited walls,
And the immortal trees which overtop
The cherubim-defended battlements?[3]

Cain surely had resentment against his brother also. Abel may
have been more successful than he. Abel seems definitely to have
been a better man. Thus the older was surpassed by the younger.
And now the Lord approved his brother's offering and not his
own. If he resented his brother already before this incident, then
that resentment was part of what was wrong with his attitude in
his offering. It was long afterward that Jesus said that if one is
offering his gift at the altar and there remembers that his brother
has something against him, he should go and be reconciled with
his brother and then come back and make the offering. But the
principle thus stated in words so long afterward was certainly
already good in the time of Cain. So now the very failure of the
offering increased the resentment of Cain. He brooded upon his
inferiority and his resentment grew.

Wrath finally caused the murder. It is stated plainly that Cain
was very angry. Perhaps this was a childhood trait which had
gone uncontrolled. Certainly he had never learned the discipline
which Epictetus later recommended: "Reckon the days in which
you have not been angry. I used to be angry every day; now
every other day; then every third and fourth day; and if you miss
it so long as thirty days, offer a sacrifice of thanksgiving to God."
Instead, Cain nursed his dark feelings until they burst out in
violent action.

What were the results of the murder? Inside Cain there was
perhaps remorse. Several students of the account think that Cain
struck indeed in anger but with no deliberate intention of mur-

der, and only slowly realized that he had actually taken the life of his brother. Certainly the full import and effect of many a wrong deed are not realized until afterward. The result outruns the intention. Again, Byron so interprets the situation as he writes this dialogue between Cain and the dying Abel:

> *Cain (after a moment's stupefaction).*
>   My hand! 't is all red, and with—
> What?
>   (*A long pause. —Looking slowly round.*)
>   Where am I? alone! Where's Abel? where
> Awake!—why liest thou so on the green earth?
> 'T is not the hour of slumber:—why so pale?
> What hast thou?—thou wert full of life this morn:
> Abel! I pray thee, mock me not! I smote
> Too fiercely, but not fatally. Ah, why
> Wouldst thou oppose me? This is mockery;
> And only done to daunt me:—'t was a blow—
> And but a blow. Stir—stir—nay, only stir!
> Why so—that's well! thou breath'st! breathe upon me!
> Oh, God! Oh, God!
>   *Abel (very faintly).*
>   What's he who speaks of God?
>   *Cain.*
> Thy murderer.
>   *Abel.*
>   Then may God forgive him! Cain,
> Comfort poor Zillah: she has but one brother
> Now.   (*Abel dies.*)
>   *Cain.*
>   And I none! Who makes me brotherless?
> His eyes are open! then he is not dead!
> Death is like sleep; and sleep shuts down our lids.
> His lips, too, are apart; why then he breathes!
> And yet I feel it not. —His heart!—his heart!—
> Let me see, doth it beat?—methinks—No!—no!
> This is a vision, else I am become
> The native of another and worse world.

The earth swims round me:—what is this? 't is wet;
    (Puts his hand to his brow, and then looks at it.)
And yet there are no dews! 'T is blood—my blood—
My brother's and my own; and shed by me!
Then what have I further to do with life,
Since I have taken his life from my own flesh?
But he cannot be dead!—Is silence death?
No; he will wake: then let me watch by him.
Life cannot be so slight, as to be quench'd
Thus quickly!—he hath spoken to me since—
What shall I say to him?—My brother!—No;
He will not answer to that name; for brethren
Smite not each other. Yet—yet—speak to me.
Oh! for a word more of that gentle voice,
That I may bear to hear my own again![4]

Fear certainly gripped Cain as well as remorse. He now feels
that whoever finds him will slay him. He will never again walk
unafraid. From now on he knows the uneasiness of the guilty
conscience so vividly described by Job:

> The bad man suffers torment all his life . . .
> Terrors are always sounding in his ears; . . .
> Of lasting through the dark hour, he despairs,
> sure that his doom is fixed,
> to be the vulture's prey,
> to perish by the sword;
> the dark days terrify him,
> anguish and agony overpower him.[5]

The chant of the chorus concerning the supposed murderer of
Laïus in the drama of Sophocles could well sound in his ears:

Who is he by voice immortal named from Pythia's rocky cell,
Doer of foul deeds of bloodshed, horrors that no tongue can tell?
    A foot for flight he needs
    Fleeter than storm-swift steeds,
    For on his heels doth follow,
Armed with the lightnings of his Sire, Apollo.
    Like sleuth-hounds too

> The Fates pursue.
> Now like a sullen bull he roves
> Through forest brakes and upland groves,
> And vainly seeks to fly
> The doom that ever nigh
> Flits o'er his head.[6]

Thus Cain staggers forth, to be henceforth a fugitive and a vagabond. The word "fugitive," which is used in the text, might be translated more exactly as a "totterer." It describes the hesitating and uncertain gait of one who does not know where to go, and who staggers on his way. So Cain dwelt in the land of Nod (which means Wandering), east of Eden.[7]

There were disastrous results in society too. The first act of murder started an unending chain of retaliation and feuding. This miserable fugitive and known criminal would be an easy prey to those he might fall among. This is what Cain feared. The Lord placed a mark on Cain for such protection as it might give him, and he said: "If any one slays Cain, vengeance shall be taken on him sevenfold."[8] Perhaps this does not represent the imposition of an arbitrary penalty, but simply the statement of the inevitable effect of the crime. Because he slew Abel, someone will slay Cain. In turn, others will rise up against this new slayer. As in the blood feuds of Arabia where the members of the family are slain as well as the guilty individual, sevenfold vengeance will be taken. Before Chapter 4 is over, we hear Lamech, the great-great-great-grandson of Cain, boasting that he slays a man for only wounding him, and takes vengeance not just sevenfold but seventy-sevenfold. This is the melancholy and bitter multiplication and proliferation of revenge and counterrevenge in the world. This is the melancholy course of events which continues even until today. Selecting an item almost at random from the daily press, in the first six months of 1960 a "startling" increase in major crimes was reported by J. Edgar Hoover, director of the Federal Bureau of

Investigation in the United States. Without repeating the statistics in all the different categories, we note this single listing: "Murders increased by 6 per cent." The dreadful deed of Cain continues to be done with increased frequency in the world.

What can we do toward the eradication of murder? It is important to inculcate respect for life. The name of Abel means "breath," as we saw. Cain extinguished the breath of life in a fellow human being and, having done so, could not undo what he had done. We can take life but we cannot restore it. Therefore in all its forms, life deserves our respect. Since in the covenant with Adam man was given dominion over the animals, and since in the covenant with Noah he was given the right to eat of the clean animals for food, it seems regrettable that in India the cow, for example, is accorded so high a place that sacred cattle wander the streets in droves while human beings starve, and that aged cows are cared for in homes for aged cows while people lie homeless on the streets. Surely it is needful to eliminate the disease-carrying insect, and to curb the predatory beast. Even a Buddhist priest is reported to have launched a fly-extermination campaign in Japan with the prayer: "Dear flies, have no rancor against us for killing you, but accept in manly fashion the inevitable consequence of being born in this world as flies." Nevertheless, there was a lamentable failure to inculcate respect for life in the case of the two boys who rowed out to a small island in San Francisco Bay and, simply for the supposed fun of it, slaughtered most of the rare and beautiful white egrets which nested there. Ponder also the report by Alan Moorehead in *No Room in the Ark* that, by the depredations of white and black man alike, 90 per cent of the wild animals of Africa have now been exterminated forever. "The chances of preserving the remaining 10 per cent seem to be a little better than they were," he writes, "and it may even be that the human instinct to kill all other living things on earth will wear itself out at last."[9]

One remembers Albert Schweitzer's famous principle of "reverence for life." Even when he was only a preschool child it seemed to him incomprehensible that he should pray for human beings only, so he composed an evening prayer for all living creatures: "O, heavenly Father, protect and bless all things that have breath; guard them from all evil, and let them sleep in peace." Long afterward, as a medical missionary in Africa, he was proceeding up a river on an errand of mercy. Seated on the deck of the barge, he was thinking—endeavoring to find some elementary and universal principle of ethics not yet discovered in any philosophy. On the third day, at sunset, while they were making their way through a herd of hippopotamuses, there suddenly flashed upon his mind in a way that he says was unforeseen and unsought, the phrase "reverence for life." This, he felt, was the idea for which he had long been seeking. When he wrote, then, about ethics, he declared: "Ethics is nothing else than reverence for life." When he confronted the tragic world struggles of our time, he made this analysis:

Today there is an absence of thinking which is characterized by a contempt of life. We waged war for questions which, through reason, might have been solved. No one won. The war killed millions of men, brought suffering to millions of men, and brought suffering and death to millions of innocent animals. Why? Because we did not possess the highest rationality of reverence for life. And because we do not yet possess this, every people is afraid of every other, and each causes fear to the others. . . . There is no other remedy than reverence for life, and at that we must arrive.[10]

The reconciliation of rivalries is also indicated as necessary. According to our analysis of Genesis 4, there is reflected here the ancient rivalry between pastoral and agricultural life. To us now it seems thoroughly possible for both modes of life to coexist. But in our day other differences constitute acute problems, and we too have to ask whether the other man must do and be and believe just the same as ourselves before we are willing to let him live. There are in the world other systems of production, of society, and of belief than our own. In the foreseeable future there is no likelihood that all will become the same. Must we then exterminate one another because of these rivalries? The warning of our story is that we may; the admonition of it is that we should not. In regard to the problem at the point where it is presently most difficult, namely, in the relations between the United States of America and the U.S.S.R., John C. Bennett recently published an analysis which could be summed up in the statement that the chances for a tolerable future are dependent upon critical and competitive, but also partly co-operative, coexistence with the Soviet Union.[11]

Reduction of armaments must also be sought. Lamech's boast of seventy-sevenfold vengeance was made just after the text mentions the forging of instruments of bronze and iron. In fact it was none other than a son of Lamech, Tubal-cain, who was credited with this invention. Was it the availability of weapons of metal, the most advanced instruments of destruction of that time, which made Lamech so bold and ruthless? Let us, then, persistently and patiently seek how we may lay down our weapons together before we destroy one another with them.

The restudy and eventual repeal of capital punishment may also be suggested. Although Cain was a known murderer, the Lord put a mark on him so that he might not be slain. He was indeed removed from the society in which he had wrought his harm, and it seems necessary that the criminal be taken apart from the society in which he has done his damage, at least until it is safe for him to be returned to it as a rehabilitated man. Indeed, when a convicted criminal is executed swiftly, but the victim of the violence he is presumed to have done sits on through the years in an insane asylum, staring with unseeing eyes out of a blank mind, destroyed by the terror of what was done, one is not sure but that the fate of the former is kinder than of the latter. Yet as long as man's justice is fallible and mistakes are made, as long as statistically capital punishment is not a deterrent to crime, and in view of the fact that God was kind even to Cain, it would seem a defensible proposition that the breath of life should not be extinguished even by the state. As an example pointing toward this conclusion, one may note that a man recently walked free out of the gates of San Quentin Prison after twenty-eight years in which his death penalty had been reprieved eight times. In the years he had finished high school and taken university work, had returned to the Roman Catholic faith of his family, had rebuilt a workshop into a Catholic chapel and served the chaplain as aide, and had helped develop one of the prison system's largest and most successful forestry honor camps. As a newspaper reporter said, it was a tranquil man who stepped into a free world, when Jack D. Green walked out of the gates of San Quentin. The conclusion of most of the participants in a United Nations' seminar on human rights held in Tokyo in 1960, that a gradual limitation of capital punishment, and its eventual abolition, are desirable, is that which has been supported here.

The revocation of licenses for drunken drivers is suggested too. The slaughter of man by man is currently at its highest on the highway. Here virtually everyone is free to proceed with machines of very great power and lethal capability. Here unavoidably accidents occur and always will despite our best intentions. But here, too, a vast number of avoidable accidents occur, caused by drinking drivers. The child, the aged pedestrian, the father of a family, the carload of nurses, killed by a drunken driver because of his drunkenness, are entirely as dead as if slain by Cain. Driving is a moral responsibility. To drink and then drive is to flout that responsibility, and should be made impossible by every means at the command of society.

Fundamental is the rooting out of the roots of murder. If our analysis was correct, Cain's act of murder began in the evil thoughts he nursed within his mind. Jesus was later to say that not the one alone who kills, but every one who is angry with his brother, shall be liable to judgment.[12] Here indeed is the beginning place, and here, therefore, is the place to begin the eradication of murder.

And yet again it is necessary to remember the ramifications of murder. Perhaps some of us are not apt to slay anyone, but did we never kill a hope nor crush an expectation? Walter Russell Bowie asks:

Who is there that has not hurt some other human being, if not with such a mortal stroke as that which Cain gave to Abel, yet in some way that has left some part of that other one's happiness and well-being lying dead? It may have been through hot passion: through lust that has defiled another life, through sudden anger that has lashed out against some supposed offense, through violence of word or act that satisfied revenge. It may have been through a colder cruelty: a sneer, a contemptuous look, a sinister disparagement that struck home like a poisoned arrow. . . . Or suppose that we never deliberately intended evil: are there no hurts we have given just because we were too stupid to understand?[13]

4 THE FLOOD (*Genesis 5:1-9:17*)

In reading the account of the deluge in Genesis 5-9, the ordinary person naturally asks, Was there really a great flood? From the inundations which must have accompanied the melting of the great glaciers at the end of the ice age ten thousand years ago, to the disaster in Chile in 1960 when earthquakes produced tidal waves that devastated the coast and rushed at four hundred miles per hour across the Pacific to wash away villages in Japan, floods have been a part of human experience upon this planet. In relation to the Bible record it would seem that we should seek for a flood which was centered where the biblical history was unfolding at the time. We remember that man lived in the garden of Eden and then went forth east of Eden, and we have already seen that the biblical localization of the area in question points to the Middle East in general and to Mesopotamia in particular. Now it is precisely in Mesopotamia that we do find flood evidences from an early period. In the excavation of a number of ancient Mesopotamian sites, layers of sediment from two to ten feet thick have been uncovered. While the evidence is possibly debatable, it has usually been thought that such a stratum represents the deposit of a major inundation. Above and below the stratum are cultural remains; the deposit marks an interruption or break in the development of civilization. Layers of this sort are found at Ur and at Nineveh, where they date probably from the fourth millennium B.C.; they occur also at Kish, Shuruppak, and Uruk, where the date is in the third millennium, perhaps around 2800 B.C. The most recent survey of this evidence has been made by André Parrot, a French archaeologist who has dug in Mesopotamia for twenty-five years. In his book *The Flood and Noah's Ark*, he says: "These strata seem to represent deposits left by more or less violent overflowings of either one or both Mesopotamian rivers. . . . I believe that one of these cataclysms was accompanied by destruction on such a scale, and made such an impression, that it became one of the themes of cuneiform literature. This was *the* Flood."[1] As to how the deluge took place, Parrot suggests that more than usually violent flooding of the Euphrates and Tigris transpired, that there were torrential rains (for even now there is rainfall in this area of a violence to which we are unaccustomed in the West), and that possibly there was at the same time a tidal wave from the Persian Gulf. Surely all of this put together would correspond well with the description in Genesis 7:11: "All the fountains of the great deep burst forth, and the windows of the heavens were opened." To inhabitants dwelling here, a catastrophe of this magnitude might well seem as if it had encompassed the whole world. As far as they were concerned, it did.

Next we ask, Where does the flood account come from? In fact, some form of flood story is to be found all around the world. In his study of comparative religions, James G. Frazer[2] collected examples of a flood story from the Near East: Mesopotamia, Palestine, and Greece; from South Asia: India, Burma, Malaya, Sumatra, and Borneo; from the Pacific: Australia and Polynesia; and from the Americas: North America, Central America, and South America. Only in China, Japan, and Africa, including

Egypt, did he not find stories of this sort. In part, one supposes that the various stories may have arisen from various flood experiences of the human race. But at least some of the stories seem to be related to one another, and one may assume that a common source lies back of at least some of them. In particular, Mesopotamian influence seems traceable at least as far east as India, and as far west as Greece. In India there are allusions to a flood story in the Vedas (1500-1000 B.C.), and such a narrative is found in the Brahmanas (1000-500 B.C.). Here Manu, the first man, befriended a small fish. In gratitude, the fish told the man that a flood was coming, but if the man would build a ship, the fish would return and rescue him. When the flood came, therefore, the fish returned and towed Manu in his ship to a mountain in the north. It is probably not accidental that the fish is the symbol of the god Ea who, in the Mesopotamian account, tells the man to build the boat. In Greece, in the middle of the first century B.C., Apollodorus tells how Zeus sent a heavy rain to destroy men. A few people escaped to the mountaintops, while the king Deukalion prepared a chest, loaded it with provisions, and, with his wife Pyrrha, took refuge in it. After nine days and nights they landed safely on Mount Parnassus. Since some persons were saved by simply going up on the mountains, it seems probable that the particular feature of floating in a chest may have come from Mesopotamia.

The Mesopotamian flood account, which may thus have been the ultimate source of at least some of the other flood stories in the world, is at any rate the oldest of them all. If the Greek story goes back to the first century B.C. or before, and the Indian tale to 1000 B.C. or earlier, the Mesopotamian account is traceable to 2000 B.C. or earlier. In the third millennium B.C., and perhaps even before, the Sumerians were the chief people in Lower Mesopotamia. By that time, writing had been invented, and the Sumerians have left us an extensive literature written with wedge-shaped marks on clay tablets. One of these cuneiform tablets, dating from at least as early as 2000 B.C., was found, broken, at Nippur, and is now in the University Museum of the University of Pennsylvania. According to this source, the gods planned to destroy mankind by a flood, but one man was told about it. When the flood came, this man rode it out in a huge boat. He must also have had animals with him, for when the sun finally shone again, he sacrificed an ox and a sheep in thanksgiving.

After the Sumerians came the Babylonians, who wrote in Akkadian, a Semitic language. A fragment of the same story, as they told it, was also found at Nippur and dates from the First Dynasty of Babylon, around 1800 B.C. This fragment records the command to build a large ship, which is called an ark and named the "Preserver of Life," and to take aboard "the beasts of the field, the fowl of the heavens." A more nearly complete form of the Babylonian account was ultimately preserved for us in the seventh-century library of Ashurbanipal at Nineveh, and it was from this source that we first learned of the existence of the Mesopotamian flood story, the much greater antiquity of which we now know from the later finds mentioned just above. Cuneiform tablets from the excavations at Nineveh were brought to the British Museum and here, in 1872, George Smith was sorting them. Suddenly he noticed a statement to the effect that a ship rested on the mountains of Nisir, and that a dove was sent forth but found no resting place and returned. He realized that he had found the flood story.

In its full form the Babylonian narrative contains nine points: (1) The gods decide to make a flood. (2) One man is warned by the deity Ea and told to build a ship. (3) In addition to his family, he is to take animals aboard. (4) The flood turns humanity into clay. (5) The ship grounds on Mount Nisir. (6) The man learns when the waters have subsided by sending out a dove, a swallow, and a raven. (7) He offers sacrifice to the gods. (8) The gods smell the sweet savor. (9) The god Enlil blesses the man and his wife.

The same sequence of nine points occurs in the flood account in the Old Testament. (1) The Lord decides to destroy wicked mankind. (2) He warns Noah and tells him to build an ark. (3) In addition to his family, Noah is to take animals aboard. (4) The flood destroys all flesh. (5) The ark comes to rest upon the mountains of Ararat. (6). Noah learns when the waters have gone down by sending out a raven and a dove. (7) He offers sacrifice to the Lord. (8) The Lord smells the pleasing odor. (9) God blesses Noah and his sons. It must, therefore, be concluded that the biblical account is related to the Mesopotamian. Could the Israelites have derived it from Mesopotamia? Yes, as Joshua 24:2 states, the ancestors of the Israelites formerly lived in Mesopotamia, where they worshiped other gods. Their descendants must have brought this story with them to Palestine and told it many times. As they did so, they omitted the polytheistic and crude features of the Mesopotamian account (although they did retain, in Genesis 8:21, the anthropomorphic expression that "the Lord smelled the pleasing odor" which, as Leviticus 26:31 shows, was a vivid type of language not infrequently used in connection with sacrifice), and they told the story in the light of their knowledge of the one God, and their understanding of his dealings with mankind. In the telling, they also gave the account in two slightly different forms, now woven together into one in our chapters of Genesis. This hypothesis of two slightly variant earlier forms of the Israelite story provides the simplest explanation of such minor divergences in the account as that one pair of unclean and seven pairs of clean animals, or one pair of all animals, were taken into the ark; and that the waters increased for forty days, or that they prevailed for one hundred and fifty days.

What kind of an account is this? It is obviously, if what we have

set forth thus far is correct, an oft-told account. It has been related
in many different lands and down through many centuries. It is
about something which took place upon earth. It is a narrative
of poetic character which intends to bring out the meaning of
what happened. Concerning the first chapter of Genesis, we
noted that the word "myth" is sometimes applied to such an
account, which tells in the language of human life about what
goes beyond human life. Concerning accounts such as the one
presently dealt with, the word "legend" is sometimes used. A
legend is an oft-told poetic account of an earthly happening. The
words "myth" and "legend" have a variety of meanings to different
people, however, and we may prefer to say simply that Genesis
begins with a sublime poem about the creative work of God, and
that it continues with vivid poetic narratives about men. Hermann
Gunkel, in fact, who is most famous for his application of the
category of legend to the early records of Genesis, is most explicit
in emphasizing this essential characteristic of these accounts. In
his book *The Legends of Genesis*, he writes:

The important point is and will remain the poetic tone of the
narratives. . . . Legend is by nature poetry, its aim being to please,
to elevate, to inspire and to move. He who wishes to do justice to
such narratives must have some aesthetic faculty, to catch in the
telling of a story what it is and what it purports to be. And in
doing so he is not expressing a hostile or even skeptical judgment,
but simply studying lovingly the nature of his material.

The conclusion . . . that one of these narratives is legend is by
no means intended to detract from the value of the narrative; it
only means that the one who pronounces it has perceived somewhat of the poetic beauty of the narrative and thinks that he has
thus arrived at an understanding of the story. Only ignorance
can regard such a conclusion as irreverent, for it is the judgment
of reverence and love. These poetic narratives are the most beautiful possession which a people brings down through the course
of its history, and the legends of Israel, especially those of Genesis,

are perhaps the most beautiful and most profound ever known on earth.[3]

What does the account in Genesis 5-9 tell? It records that mankind degenerated. According to Chapter 5 there was a long time from Adam until the flood, and we may call this the antediluvian period. The way the Sumerians looked at this period may be seen in the Sumerian King List, a cuneiform document of around 2000 B.C. Here there is a list of eight antediluvian kings, who ruled in five different cities, and whose combined reigns covered a period of 241,200 years. In another form of the list there were ten kings and their reigns covered 432,000 years. Interestingly enough, the Old Testament also reckons ten generations down to the flood. The antediluvian patriarchs of Genesis 5 are: Adam, Seth (who must have been born after the murder of Abel and, to a certain extent, took the place of Abel), Enosh, Kenan, Mahalalel, Jared, Enoch, Methuselah, Lamech, and Noah. The total of their years, according to the Hebrew text, is 1656. Jules Oppert, a French Orientalist, made an ingenious suggestion to explain how these figures were arrived at. The Sumerians and Babylonians had a sexagesimal system of arithmetic, in which the reckoning was by 60's. We are still under their influence in that we count 60 seconds, 60 minutes, and 360 degrees. Now 60 seconds times 60 minutes times 24 hours equals 86,400 seconds in a day (a unit used now in the tracking of the satellites). Those peoples also employed a unit of 60 months, which equals five years, and 86,400 times 5 years equals 432,000 years. But the Israelites took the week as their unit instead of the period of five years, and 86,400 times 7 days equals 604,800 days, which is 1656 years. Whether or not this is the correct explanation of the origin of the two sets of figures, it is evident that as they looked back into what must have been the dimly remembered past, both the Sumerians and the Israelites pictured a long antediluvian period.

In comparison with the extravagant figures assigned to the personages of that period by the Sumerians, the figures given by the Israelites are relatively modest.

In this long antediluvian period civilization advanced. The Babylonians said that in this time the gods came and taught all kinds of sciences and arts, such as writing, city and temple building, and legislation. The Old Testament records, for its part, that Cain and Abel began the occupations of agriculture and pastoral work, that Enoch built a city, and that of the sons of Lamech, Jubal originated the profession of music, while Tubal-cain invented the forging of metal.

But in this long period mankind also went from bad to worse. Cain inaugurated murder, Lamech introduced polygamy, and supernatural beings and mortal women formed unnatural marriage alliances. Finally, in Genesis 6:5 we read that "the Lord saw that the wickedness of man was great in the earth, and that every imagination of the thoughts of his heart was only evil continually." God was sorry that he had made man.

Next, the account tells that disaster came. Genesis 6-8 describes this disaster which came in the form of the great flood.

And, after that, a new departure was made. This is described in Genesis 9:1-17. In the original order of things there was harmony in all creation. Slaughter in all its forms was prohibited. Man had dominion over other living creatures, but he did not slay them. Plants yielding seed, and trees with fruit, provided his sustenance, and the beasts and birds, too, had every green plant for food. But by now "all flesh had corrupted their way upon the earth," as Genesis 6:12 states. The animals had commenced to prey upon one another, and to attack man. Man slew the animals, which lived now in dread of him, and man slew his fellow man. It was no longer possible to return to paradise, but at least on a less ideal level a new start could be made. So a new constitution was given. The slaughter of animals for human food was legalized, but two restrictions were placed upon the bloodthirsty instincts of men and animals: (1) Man was not to eat the blood with the flesh; and (2) human blood was not to be shed with impunity by either beast or man. These were the obligations laid upon all men and animals, and along with the requirements went the promise of God never again to destroy all flesh in a great flood. Of that promise the rainbow, which shines after every storm, is a sign. Such was the covenant with Noah, and such was the new departure which was made.

What does this account teach? It is the aim of a poetic narrative, as Hermann Gunkel said, "to elevate, to inspire and to move." This account elevates our thought about God. He is a God of judgment and of mercy. The flood was a judgment upon a degenerate race. Disasters may come from natural causes, but they fall upon sinful man as moral judgments. Of this account, Walter Russell Bowie writes:

The ancient story . . . is a parable . . . of terrible reality. There can be a point in the disintegration due to evil when something has to break. Then the forces of decency left on earth are not strong enough to hold back the pressure of moral consequence. It will rain upon the earth not only for forty days, as in the story of Noah, but for four years as in World War I, and more than four years, as in World War II; and the wash and welter of it may prevail not only "a hundred and fifty days," but through dragging decades in which the aftermath of war still spreads its slime of bitterness and suffering. And the flood is not of water only; it is, and in every recurring judgment it must be, of blood and tears.[4]

Yet after the judgment, humanity was started on its course afresh, with new promises and new blessings. The first sign of promise was the single olive leaf which the dove brought back, yet a single leaf is a sign that the restorative power of the merciful God is still at work.

This account inspires our thought about man. In that day the earth was filled with violence, and so it has been in our day too. Yet in that day there was a righteous man. Of Noah it is said that he found favor in the sight of God, and he is characterized as righteous and blameless. In particular it is said of him that he walked with God. This is the Old Testament expression for the religious life. This man formed the habit of conversing with God, and of going in his ways. Even when God gave him the surprising and hard command to build the ark, he obeyed. The presence of such a man, even in a degenerate world, is an inspiring fact.

And the account moves us to action. On the very day of the deluge, as the rain began to fall, Noah went aboard the ship, and his three sons, Shem, Ham, and Japheth, and his wife and the three wives of his sons, and all the animals. The ark was a great and seaworthy vessel. In the Babylonian version it is a seven-storied cube. In the Old Testament description it is of relative dimensions comparable to a modern ship. These dimensions are stated in the unit of the cubit, which was the length from the elbow to the fingertips, or about one and one-half feet. The length of the ark was 300 cubits, or about 450 feet, nearly half the length of the steamship *Queen Mary*. The breadth was 50 cubits, that is, the beam was about 75 feet. The height was 30 cubits, or about 45 feet. The ark was divided into lower, second, and third decks. An Arabic manuscript in the Convent of Saint Catherine at Mount Sinai states that the beasts and cattle were in the hold, the birds on the number two deck, and the human beings on the top deck. There the men were on one side, the women on the other, and the corpse of Adam, exhumed for the occasion, made a barrier in the middle. In the ark they all floated safely upon the flood, and at last they came to rest upon 17,000-foot Mount Ararat.

When Noah led his party aboard, one wonders how many people stood outside, scoffed and laughed, and remained to perish? There is reason to think that even one relative of Noah himself, who presumably would have been welcome on board, did not choose to go and stayed behind to die. This was none other than Noah's grandfather, whose name was Methuselah. The reason for this conclusion concerning Methuselah is as follows: Methuselah was 187 years of age when his son Lamech was born, Lamech was 182 when Noah was born, and Noah was 600 when the flood came. This totals 969 years, and Genesis 5:27 states that Methuselah was 969 years old when he died. Therefore, he died in the year of the flood, and probably in the flood.

At any rate it was only a few who were saved, but their deliverance was wonderful. In a later time, I Peter 3:20 recalls how in the days of Noah, in the ark, a few, that is eight persons, were saved through water, and then observes that Christian baptism corresponds to this. In the Christian catacombs the picture of Noah in the ark was often painted, as a symbol of salvation. The church fathers saw the ark as the figure of the church. In it we are carried safe across the stormy sea. In 1713, in his *History of the Old and New Testaments with Edifying Examples,* le Maistre de Sacy wrote of the ark:

The mighty size of this construction which was borne upon the water, and this assembly of all manner of clean and unclean beasts, represented the extent of the Church throughout all the earth, and the calling of many nations and peoples differing among themselves in the diversity of their habits and customs, whom God, whose will it is that all men should be saved, would one day join together in this refuge, in order that they might find a like salvation and escape a like shipwreck.

The wood and the water visibly represent two great mysteries: the water, that Baptism which washes us clean of sin, as the Flood purified the world of its abominations; and the wood of the Cross of the Saviour, who has saved the whole world, and who is still today the only hope of Christian folk, who look for salvation only through its infinite cost. Thus did it please God to prefigure His Church in that Ark, which served for the mending and re-newing of the world. And we ought always to render to God our thanks that He has brought us into it, to save us from the Flood of sin and transgressions which inundates the whole earth.[5]

Yes, in our day, too, the clouds are darkening. The first drops of rain are coming down. But the ark of salvation is on the ways. The door is still open. Let us come aboard before it is too late.

5 NOAH AND HIS WINE

(Genesis 9:18-29)

Noah landed the ark on Mount Ararat. After that he planted a vineyard, drank of the wine, and became drunken. As he lay there in his stupor, one of his sons despised him, but the other two respectfully covered him up. When he realized what had happened, he cursed the one son and son's son, and blessed the other two.

What were the reasons for Noah's drinking? Some of the reasons were probably environmental. Noah had been on a sea voyage. I do not think that Noah had liquor on board the ark. It is true that in *The Green Pastures* Noah asked "de Lawd" if he might take two kegs of whiskey, and put one on each side to balance the ship, but was told he should take only one and put it in the middle. That is in a play, however, and the Bible does not appear to allow such a representation. In the biblical order of events, Noah's drinking comes only after the flood. Furthermore, we note that in the flood Noah actually made his landfall and got his ship safely anchored on Mount Ararat. As the mariner and navigator of a large ship I doubt if he could have done that if he had been intoxicated. Nevertheless, he had just been on this sea voyage, and there seems to be something about a sea voyage and ships and boats that is conducive to drinking. The first time the present writer went across the Atlantic by ship was in the days of prohibition in the United States of America. This was when for a short time it was decided that instead of just being sorry that there were so many crimes, auto accidents, broken families, and suicides, something should actually be done to remove one of the chief causes of such happenings. To many people this appeared arbitrary, and they felt they suffered a great repression. So on this sea voyage the people who were so repressed on land could not wait to get beyond the three-mile limit to make up for the deprivations which they had been suffering. There was a doctor who assuredly knew from his medical training the physiological effects of drink, but it did not save him from exhibiting those effects. There was a young man who in the name of his personal liberty to drink thought, wrongly, that he could infringe upon my personal liberty not to. One notices also that the cargo loaded on smaller pleasure boats, which have become so numerous in the United States, often includes alcoholic drinks, and that soon thereafter the persons on board begin to exhibit greater than usual hilarity. So when one recalls that Noah had been so long on shipboard and at sea, one supposes that this environmental factor may have been an influence on him.

He was also now in a foreign country. The ark came down on Mount Ararat, which is in what is now called Armenia, far north of Palestine. In a foreign land like that one cannot be sure of the water. One gets very tired of always drinking hot tea. So one almost has to order wine, and if one orders wine one might as well order something stronger. Anyway, when one is in Rome one should do as the Romans do. The further problem, of course, is that we are mostly in Rome right here at home, too. In a fraternity one would not want to be unfraternal, would one? In a restaurant one would not dare to offend the haughty waiter, would one?

What would a cocktail party be if there were no cocktails? Obviously a contradiction in terms. On the street one can generally find half a dozen liquor stores before one can find a dairy store. Generally water is hard to come by even at a church dinner, and generally anywhere outside of a church liquor is easy to get.

It was also the case that Noah had been at a high altitude. Great Ararat is the highest peak of the Ararat Mountains, and is 16,916 feet high. At 17,000 feet one cannot be without liquor very long. In fact, the higher one gets the less long one can be without it. At 37,000 feet a commercial jet flies from San Francisco to New York City in five hours. But at that altitude one could not make it unsupported that long. Therefore, liquor must be served on board. Of course the patrons might bring their own, but so many were doing that and were making disturbances that corrective measures had to be taken. Thirty-five cases were recently cited to the Senate Interstate Commerce Committee in which serious emergencies were created by intoxicated passengers, and the president of the Air Line Pilots Association was quoted as saying: "The time of the crew in these high speed, complex aircraft is fully occupied with flight duties and should not be spent in playing nursemaid to inebriated passengers." Therefore, the Federal Aviation Agency had to take notice of the danger in flight and, since it obviously would not do to deprive anyone of his drinks for as long as five hours, it was ruled that all drinks must be served by stewardesses, even if they just poured back for him what the passenger had carried on board, and that they must police the amount consumed and the unruliness of the consumers. Whereupon the glamorous profession of the airline stewardess became by government ruling this much less attractive. As to the flight crew, not even Mr. Schenley, Mr. Schlitz, or Mr. Sky Blue Waters wants to fly with an inebriated pilot, and so here some rules, even arbitrary ones, are actually enforced.

These, then, seem to have been some environmental circumstances in the life of Noah—a sea voyage, an experience in a foreign land, and a high-altitude trip—which led to his drinking; at any rate, similar factors seem to be potent forces to lead many to drink today.

Other reasons for Noah's drinking, however, appear to have been psychological. That is, they were forces not outside Noah but inside himself. For one thing, there was curiosity. Noah had never had a drink. In fact nobody ever had. In the Revised Standard Version, Genesis 9:20 reads: "Noah was the first tiller of the soil. He planted a vineyard." That is not true, however, for already in Genesis 4:2 Cain was a tiller of the ground, and it is Cain who is credited with the beginning of the practice of agriculture. Therefore, the translation of the verse given by John Skinner in *The International Critical Commentary* is probably correct: "Noah the husbandman was the first who planted a vineyard."[1] Like Cain before him, Noah was a farmer, and the new thing which he did for the first time ever was to plant a vineyard. According to the context, this must have been up near Mount Ararat, in Armenia. In his commentary on Genesis, S. R. Driver states that Armenia and adjacent Pontus are precisely the region in which the vine appears to be indigenous and from which it spread gradually to other countries.[2] So Noah was the first one who ever did this. He planted a vineyard. He harvested the grapes. He enjoyed the good, healthful grapejuice. He kept some of it too long. It spoiled. He said to himself: "It is fermented! It is aged! I wonder how it would taste now, and how it would make me feel?" Proverbs had not yet been written, which says in 23:31, "Do not look at wine when it is red, when it sparkles in the cup," so Noah did not have anyone to warn him. I think his curiosity got the better of him, as it may of anyone who has not yet had his first drink and is wondering what it would taste like.

There was also a desire for relaxation. One can scarcely imagine what a strain Noah had been under. He had been responsible, with a very small crew and a very heavy cargo, for a vessel nearly half the size of the *Queen Mary*. He had gone through what, as a plain statement of fact, was the worst storm the world had ever seen. Would one not want to let down a little? Added to the major hazards were the minor irritations, which are often the hardest to bear. One writer expressed sympathy for the plight of Noah in these words:

> My heart goes out to poor old Noah,
> Feeding leopards, watching boa,
> Reassuring a hippo mother,
> Keeping his charges from eating each other,
> For having started two by two
> One by one would be too few.
> No wonder he seethed in helpless rage
> After all that time in an animal cage![3]

Relaxation, of a sort, is provided by alcohol. The sort of relaxation it provides is a kind of numbness and stupefaction. In fact, alcohol is properly classified as a narcotic in the general sense of that term. The word "narcotic" is derived from a Greek term which means "to benumb." Contrary to popular opinion, the fundamental effect of alcohol is not to energize but to slow and weaken the activities of the mind and the body. Dr. Richard C. Cabot states: "Alcohol is always a narcotic, never a stimulant, and therefore has none of the uses ordinarily attributed to it."[4] A person who is drinking moves about more and becomes noisier not because he has been stimulated but only because the first effect of alcohol is to act upon the higher parts of the brain and to remove his inhibitions. In anesthesia there is also an early stage of excitement before the patient quiets down and goes to sleep, and alcohol was in fact one of the first anesthetics ever known.[5] So Noah was using a primitive anesthetic to get relaxation, and when the sons found him stretched out in his tent he was certainly relaxed. People still want relaxation after strain, and find drinking an obvious way to get it. In his day Eugene V. Debs, a founder of the Industrial Workers of the World and a Socialist party candidate for the presidency of the United States of America, seems to have been a glamorous and influential person. One of the men who traveled with him on his lecture tours wrote of him:

In my opinion Eugene Debs had an unusually high type of brain—so nicely adjusted that a tablespoonful of whiskey would give all the effects of a bottle. In my judgment he only got really drunk when alone, after a long strain. Twice I know, when his tour of dates had been filled, he disappeared for weeks—presumably on a batter. All over the country the reporters seemed to have an unwritten rule to say nothing of the habit, out of admiration for him.[6]

Likewise a young man, for whom drinking was becoming a problem, said to me recently: "I want to relax. The bar is dark and cool, and I sit down. And of course I take a drink."

Closely related to the psychological factor to which we have just referred is the further one of desire for escape. Environment can suggest that one take a drink, and curiosity can lead one to try it, but it really gets hold of a person when he finds that drinking provides an escape from things which otherwise are too much for him. Some of us want to escape from our memories. Perhaps Noah wished to escape from the remembrance of the intolerable racket of all the animals cooped up in the ark, and the towering waves which threatened to overwhelm him. Some of us want to escape from our responsibilities which may be monotonous and wearisome. Noah was back from the sea, and he had the drudgery of running a farm. The ark was fast aground, and the vineyard was probably full of weeds. Lamech his father had said hopefully in Genesis 5:29 about Noah: "Out of the ground which the Lord has cursed this one shall bring us relief from our work and from the toil of our hands." Unfortunately, the relief from work and toil which Noah found in drinking wine made his toil and work harder than ever when he went back to it. The escape which alcohol provides is always a spurious escape, and the reality to which one returns afterward is always a little harder to deal with than it was before. Nevertheless, the desire to evade hard reality still draws men to drink. Jack London came home from the sea and took a job in Oakland, California, in a steam laundry. When Saturday night came, he had to drink to get away from it. He wrote: "I, the long-time intimate of John Barleycorn, knew just what he promised me—maggots of fancy, dreams of power, forgetfulness, anything and everything save whirling washers, revolving mangles, humming centrifugal wringers, and fancy starch, and interminable processions of Dutch trousers moving in steam under my flying iron."

What were the results of Noah's drinking? Drinking changed the personality of Noah. Indeed, the Noah of this story is so different from the upright hero of the flood story that some of the critics think these were really two different men. But did you ever see a man made literally into a different man by drink? Here is a kind and lovable person, a friend to small boys and an expert in his profession, but when he is drinking the sheriff in a frontier town has to shut him in a padded cell. There is Noah on the bridge of the ark, taking his bearings, holding the wheel against the mountainous seas, clear-eyed and resolute. And there is this disheveled, dissolute drunk! Can that be one and the same man? Yes, unfortunately, this is precisely the difference which drink can make. How, specifically, does alcohol change a man? Drawing upon well-known and well-attested medical facts, we may say: Alcohol increases fatigue, interferes with the control and action of every muscle in the body, slows the reaction time of the nervous system, interferes with co-ordination, dulls the senses, attacks first of all the higher parts of the brain which have to do with judgment, reason, and control of behavior, and in more extreme cases shortens life and causes insanity.

As another result, Noah's drinking may have contributed to immorality. This unpleasant subject may be passed with a single quotation from the exegesis by Cuthbert A. Simpson in *The Interpreter's Bible*: "In the primary, popular form of the story there probably occurred here—as shown by the reference in vs. 24 to what his youngest son had done to him—an account of an indecent attack by Canaan on his father."[8] This, Simpson thinks, a later writer omitted from motives of delicacy.

Furthermore, Noah's drinking disrupted his family. This father wakened from his stupor to curse his son and grandson. The heaviest curse that has lain upon many a family has been that of drink, which has wasted its money and made one or more of its members a burden rather than a help. Soon after the death of his father, Upton Sinclair wrote a novel called *Love's Pilgrimage*. It opened with this description:

It was the Highway of Lost Men.
They shivered, and drew their shoulders together as they walked, for it was night, and a cold, sleety rain was falling. The lights from saloons and pawnshops fell upon their faces—faces haggard and gaunt with misery, or bloated with disease. Some stared before them fixedly; some gazed about with furtive and hungry eyes as they shuffled on. . . .
Down this highway walked a lad, about fifteen years of age, pale of face. His overcoat was buttoned tightly about his neck, and his hands thrust into his pockets; he gazed around him swiftly as he walked. He came to this place every now and then, but he never grew used to what he saw. . . .
At last, in a dingy bar-room, with saw-dust strewn upon the floor, and the odor of stale beer and tobacco-smoke in the air— here suddenly the boy sprang forward, with a cry: "Father!" And a man who sat with bowed head in a corner gave a start, and lifted a white face and stared at him. The man rose unsteadily

to his feet, and staggered to the other; and fell upon his shoulder sobbing. . . .

So they would go out, arm in arm; and while they made their progress up the Highway, the man would pour out his remorse, and tell the story of his weeks of horror.

Then, after a mile or so, he would halt. . . .

"What is it, Father?"

"I must have something to drink."

"No, Father! . . ."

And so they would fight it out—all the way back to the lodging house where they lived, and where the mother sat and wept. And here they would put him to bed . . . and tend him until he was on his feet again. Then, with clothing newly-brushed and face newly-shaven, he would go back to the world of men; and the boy would go back to his dreams.[9]

The story which began like that was a story which Upton Sinclair and his own family lived. It is a story of the disruption of a family that is as old as Noah and as new as today.

What, then, is the right thing to do about drinking? In relation to the victims of drink there are essentially but two attitudes, and these were manifested by the sons of Noah. One is the attitude of Ham, who was crude and cruel. He looked, probably snickered, perhaps took advantage, and went out and spread the story. The other is the attitude of Shem and Japheth. They showed pity and kindness. They averted their gaze, covered the shame, and waited to help.

In relation to ourselves, as we have to decide what to do on the issue of drinking, almost everybody will surely agree that the story of Noah and his wine stands as a warning. S. R. Driver writes: "The scene is a typical one; and it stands as a warning of the consequences of excessive indulgence, and of the need of watchfulness and self-control, even in the use of what is good and innocent in itself."[10]

But how shall we apply the warning? What shall we decide to do about the matter? Here too there are essentially but two opinions. The first is the opinion that it is right to drink in moderation. Biblical basis can be adduced in support of this opinion. John Skinner writes: "The moderate use of wine is certainly not condemned in the Old Testament."[11] In the New Testament, the advice contained in I Timothy 5:23 is familiar: "No longer drink only water, but use a little wine for the sake of your stomach and your frequent ailments." Also in some parts of the church this is the teaching which is given. Thus James A. Pike, now Bishop Pike, says in his book *Beyond Anxiety* that man has the responsibility of bringing to greater perfection the possibilities which already exist in nature, and he cites fermentation (which according to our story must be credited to Noah) and distillation (which was invented in the thirteenth century) as among the more interesting of these possibilities. Then he writes:

The resulting alcoholic beverages are not evil in themselves any more than nuclear fission is evil in itself. The evaluation has to be made in larger terms. . . . The cocktail hour can be a time of real renewal: we can be lifted out of the ruts into which the day has taken us, our imaginations can be inspired, our vision cleared. This gift can help break down the barriers between people, can make introverts more extrovert. A martini before dinner can put a new face on things, enabling those who have evening tasks to approach them with more freshness. Steins of beer can enhance the late evening college "bull-session." Just the right wine can dignify a course at dinner and play its part in the glory of an evening.[12]

The church leader just quoted also takes a clear position about the dangers of alcohol, expresses a vindication of those who do not drink at all (for various reasons), and states that moderation (and, for some, abstinence) is called for under the doctrine of vocation. In spite of these qualifications, it is plain that it is essentially the idea of moderate drinking which is here eloquently supported. This is also the idea which is promulgated most widely and as persuasively as possible by what appear to be the most expensive advertisements in the "finest" magazines and the many advertisements on radio and television. The pressure of these and a thousand other forces, obvious and subtle, is constantly upon us, and they all say to us: Drink, in moderation of course, but drink; it is the gracious, hospitable, sociable, distinguished, accepted thing to do.

If the present writer ventures to disagree with this widespread opinion and to say that he does not think that moderate drinking is the right solution to the problem, it is because he observes that this way has been tried and has too often brought bad results. It has been tried individually. Jack London claimed to follow precisely this way. After many years of following it, as he thought —for he claimed not to be a drunkard—he wrote a book called *John Barleycorn.* In this book he simply said that he was going to continue to follow this way better than ever. This was his conclusion:

> Mine is no tale of a reformed drunkard. I was never a drunkard, and I have not reformed. . . .
> No . . . I shall take my drink on occasion. With all the books on my shelves, with all the thoughts of the thinkers shaded by my particular temperament, I have decided coolly and deliberately that I should continue to do what I have been trained to want to do. I will drink—but oh, more skillfully, more discreetly than ever before. Never again will I be a peripatetic conflagration.

So he went on for two or three years more and then, at the age of forty, as his friend Upton Sinclair, to whom he had been a hero, says, "he gave his last word on the subject of liquor by taking his own life."[13] In the same book, entitled *The Cup of Fury,* in which he makes this report on Jack London, Upton Sinclair gives his own list of no less than seventy-five persons, thirty known to most literate Americans, a dozen known throughout the literate world, all of whom were destroyed by alcohol. Sinclair writes:

Look at the list of some of the people whose stories we've seen in this book. These were men and women the world needed—needed until they were seventy, eighty, ninety years of age. Jack London, George Sterling, O. Henry, Stephen Crane, Finley Peter Dunne, Eugene Debs, Sinclair Lewis, Isadora Duncan, William Seabrook, Edna St. Vincent Millay, George Cram Cook, Dylan Thomas, Sherwood Anderson—great people, these, with God-given power to use their minds and bodies for the betterment of our world. When they should have been enjoying their fame, and feeling warm pride at their contributions, they suffered instead.[14]

The way of moderate drinking has been tried not only individually but on a national scale. Ever since the brief experiment of prohibition was abandoned, and now for many years, this has been the most powerfully promoted way in the United States of America. It has been accepted, according to the book *Drinking in the Colleges*, by 74 per cent of the college students, who drink. It has been accepted, according to the statistics for 1960, by 70 million persons in the United States, who drink. And the results? The same statistics state that there are now 5 million alcoholics in the United States, with 200,000 more added each year. In 1960, Dr. Joel Fort, director of the Alcoholic Rehabilitation Clinic of Alameda County, California, declared in an Institute on Alcoholism at Mills College, Oakland, according to press report: "The problem of alcoholism in this country now outranks every other public health issue in terms of potential damage to individuals." Therefore, the present writer does not think this way works very well, and does not think you would think so if you had to try to help someone to whom drinking had become a problem or a disease, or if you had to live with someone like that, or if you had to be someone like that.

The other way, therefore, and the only other way available, is to leave drinking alone. The biblical basis for this is the vow of the Nazirite, found in Numbers 6, to separate himself from wine and strong drink. It is perhaps no accident that it is this same chapter which closes with the benediction that includes the words: "The Lord lift up his countenance upon you, and give you peace." It is also perhaps no accident that the strongest man in the Bible, Samson, had this vow.

The scientific basis for the same decision lies in the established facts about what alcohol is and does. It has already been pointed out above that alcohol is a narcotic in the general sense that it is a substance which tends to produce numbness and stupefaction in the body and mind. Alcohol is also a poison, which means a substance which is injurious and even deadly. Dr. Haven Emerson attests the correctness of the following facts:[15] One to two tenths of one per cent of alcohol in the blood flushes the face, causes loss of self-restraint, and disturbs the finer muscular movements. Two to three tenths of one per cent of alcohol in the blood causes unsteadiness, confuses the speech, and often makes one quarrelsome, abusive, and vulgar. More than three tenths of one percent of alcohol in the blood produces signs of more complete anesthesia and of paralysis. More than four tenths of one per cent of alcohol in the blood usually results in complete unconsciousness. More than five tenths of one per cent of alcohol in the blood brings danger of death from acute alcoholic poisoning. The conclusion seems obvious that any of the narcotic and poison called alcohol is too much.

In answer, therefore, to the question as to what is the right thing to do about drinking, we conclude: If you do not drink, do not start. If you have started, stop. If you cannot stop, ask for help to stop. Of the human agencies which try to help persons to stop, Alcoholics Anonymous seems the most successful. The first principles of Alcoholics Anonymous are to acknowledge that we cannot handle the problem by ourselves, and to ask for help from a Power greater than ourselves.

6 THE FAMILY OF MAN (*Genesis 10*)

What does Genesis 10 tell and teach? It tells that there was a large family upon earth. This was the family of Noah after the flood. Noah survived the flood with his wife and his three sons and their wives. This chapter begins with the names of the three sons given, presumably, in the order of their age, Shem, Ham, and Japheth. Then it tells us that these sons in turn had further descendants. The remainder of the chapter is occupied with listing in systematic order those descendants. The three sons are now taken in reverse order, presumably to rise to a climax with the one most important in Bible history, namely, Shem. Japheth, the youngest of the three sons, is mentioned first, and we are told that he had seven sons: Gomer, Magog, Madai, Javan, Tubal, Meshech, and Tiras. Of these sons, in turn, Gomer had three sons whose names are given, and Javan had four sons whose names are given. There were accordingly fourteen descendants of Japheth. Next we are told about the middle son Ham. He had four sons: Cush, Egypt, Put, and Canaan. In turn Cush had six sons, and one of them gave him two grandsons. Egypt likewise had seven sons, and Canaan had eleven sons. That makes thirty descendants of Ham. Finally we come to Shem, the eldest of the three sons of Noah. He had five sons: Elam, Asshur, Arpachshad, Lud, and Aram. Aram had four sons. Arpachshad had one son, one grandson, two great-grandsons, and thirteen great-great-grandsons. That makes twenty-six descendants of Shem. Of the three sons there are in all seventy descendants. Thus we have a picture of the family of Noah in seven generations, with three sons, sixteen grandsons, thirty-six great-grandsons, three great-great-grandsons, two great-great-great-grandsons, and thirteen great-great-great-great-grandsons. There was indeed a large family upon earth. It was the family of Noah.

But when we look more closely we see that Genesis 10 is also telling us that this large family was mankind. At first sight the list appears to be of individual persons. As in the case of Nimrod who is described as having been a great hunter and who evidently had a personal reputation for prowess in this field, many of the names may have been those of individuals. But some of the names are of places and of peoples. Place names are Tarshish (vs. 4), which was probably in South Spain; Sidon (vs. 15), which was on the Phoenician coast of Palestine; and Ophir (vs. 29), which may have been in India. Countries mentioned are: Cush, Egypt, and Canaan (vs. 6). Peoples are the Jebusite, the Amorite, and the Girgashite (vs. 16) and, in the Hebrew plural, the Kittim (vs. 4), the Ludim (vs. 13), and the Caphtorim (vs. 14). At least to some extent, therefore, individuals' names are used to represent and personify peoples and nations. The technical term for a name which is applied to a people or group in this way is "eponym." Thus John Skinner writes in *The International Critical Commentary* concerning this passage:

The names in the Table are throughout eponymous: that is to say, each nation is represented by an imaginary personage bearing its name, who is called into existence for the purpose of expressing its unity, but is at the same time conceived as its real progenitor. From this it was an easy step to translate the supposed affinities of the various peoples into the family relations of father, son, brother, etc., between the eponymous ancestors; while the origin of the existing ethnic groups was held to be accounted for by the expansion and partition of the family. This vivid and concrete mode of representation, though it was prevalent in antiquity, was inevitably suggested by one of the commonest idioms of Semitic speech, according to which the individual members of a tribe or people were spoken of as "sons" or "daughters" of the collective entity to which they belonged.[1]

This table, therefore, not only tells us about the large family of Noah, but by doing so gives us a picture of the peoples of the known ancient world as seen from the standpoint of the biblical writers. The area in view is the whole Mediterranean and Middle East. To the north and west dwell the sons of Japheth. Their territories extend from the Caspian Sea to the Atlantic Ocean. They include Madai, which is the common Hebrew name for Media and the Medes, the first Aryan people to appear in Asian history; and Javan, which means the Ionian Greeks in Asia Minor, and his son Tarshish, probably a place in South Spain colonized from the eastern Mediterranean. These peoples in the north and west, who are pictured as the sons of Japheth, we would call the Indo-Europeans.

In the south live the sons of Ham. They inhabit and populate Africa, South Arabia, and Canaan. Cush is the land south of Egypt, on up the Nile, which we call Nubia and which the Greeks called Ethiopia. Mizraim is the common Semitic name of Egypt. The Revised Standard Version translates it directly as Egypt, and all who have flown in Egypt recognize it as a part of the name of the national airline Mizrair. Canaan is Palestine, the land of the Canaanites and Phoenicians. Even in the northern Phoenician ruins one can still see obelisks and other objects revealing strong Egyptian influence; it is probably this close connection between Egypt and Canaan which led to making the latter a son of Ham. Sons and grandsons of Cush are: Seba, probably the place of this name mentioned by Strabo,[2] on the African side of the Red Sea; Sheba, probably the famous kingdom of this name in South Arabia; and Dedan, perhaps in North Arabia. Sons of Canaan are his firstborn Sidon, the oldest Phoenician city; Heth, meaning the Hittites; and the Jebusites, the ancient inhabitants of Jerusalem. These are the Hamitic peoples.

To the east dwell the sons of Shem. Their territory extends from beyond the Persian Gulf nearly to Asia Minor. Elam lies east of Babylonia; Asshur is the land of Assyria; Aram includes all of Syria. The sons of Shem are the Semitic peoples.

Thus the family in Genesis 10 is the mankind of the known world of the biblical author. The descendants of Noah, he tells us, spread across the earth, and the known peoples of the earth were the members and the branches of that family.

What the tenth chapter of Genesis teaches us, therefore, can be arrived at by putting together the two statements already made. First, there was a large family. Second, the family was mankind. Therefore, mankind is a family.

The next question which may arise is, Is this true? Is mankind one family? In our day we would doubtless wish to ask what science says on this matter. The relevant science would be anthropology. This science is generally considered to have been founded by Johann Friedrich Blumenbach, who was a professor at Göttingen University around 1800. In his studies he used comparative anatomy and craniometrical research. Whereas the geographical area involved in the biblical view was that which we have described above, in modern times the entire planet must be taken into account. Here again, following upon the work of Blumenbach, we commonly speak, much as the Bible account did, of three major groups of people. They are characterized as follows: (1) Caucasian: skin light, hair fair to black, and soft, straight or wavy, skull variable, nose narrow, teeth small; (2) Mongolian: complexion yellowish, hair straight and black, cheekbones prominent, eyes with a slant appearance; (3) Negroid: complexion dark brown or black, hair curly, stature tall.

Interestingly enough, within the Caucasian group, three divisions are recognized which correspond with the three family branches described in Genesis 10. Here the index is primarily linguistic. The peoples of the first division speak the Indo-European languages: Sanskrit, Greek, Latin, French, German, and English. The peoples of the second division speak the Hamitic languages: Egyptian, Coptic, Ethiopian, and North African. The peoples of the third division speak the Semitic languages: Babylonian, Aramaic, Hebrew, and Arabic. These are respectively the Japhitic, Hamitic, and Semitic peoples of the Bible record.

Granted, however, that science describes mankind in terms of such groups as these, does it, like the Bible, say that they are all of one family? To the best of our knowledge, the answer to this question is, Yes. Even though it is including peoples not only of light skin but also of yellowish and of dark skin, and even though it is using technical terminology far different from the story language of the Bible, science also affirms that these branches of mankind are all parts of one family. In *The Direction of Human Evolution*, Conklin writes: "Systematists generally agree that there is at present but one species of man, namely, *homo sapiens*, and that all races and varieties have arisen in the first instance from a common human stock."[3] At a scientific congress on race, Von Luschan declared: "Fair and dark races, long and short-headed, intelligent and primitive, all come from one stock."[4] Benjamin E. Mays points out that science has demonstrated that there are four types of blood, called O, A, B, and AB, and that an African Negro, an American white man, an Indian American, an Englishman, a Chinese, or a Japanese, each has one of the four.[5] As quoted in the press on the occasion of a public speech, Dr. Thomas Dooley, the splendid American, said: "I have examined many sick children in America, in Africa, and in Asia. I have been struck by the fact that all of these children have hearts, lungs, kidneys and other organs that are absolutely identical—that even the pattern of veins on the back of their hands is the same the world over. We are all made on the same pattern, and we are molded in the same image."

What the Bible says in one way and science in another, common experience also says to us if we have eyes to see. At the Museum of Modern Art in New York City a few years ago Edward Steichen brought together an unusual photographic exhibition called The Family of Man.[6] Looking at those pictures, one saw mankind, multitudinous and solitary, growing and dying, toiling and playing, in strife and in contentment, in joy and in sorrow, and one received a memorable impression of the unity of human experience. One felt that it is really true that all men constitute one ramified, variegated, far-flung, but essentially homogeneous family.

Thus far we have stated that Genesis, Chapter 10, teaches that all mankind is one family, and that this is true, not only as a tenet of biblical doctrine, but also as an affirmation of science and of human experience. Now what conclusion does the chapter lead to? The conclusion is relatively simple to state but not easy to implement. The conclusion, which appears obvious, is that since all mankind is one family, the members ought to treat one another like members of a family.

Since mankind is a family the members of the family ought to be able to eat together. A family ordinarily does so. But in 1960 when James M. Lawson, Jr., a Negro student in Vanderbilt University Divinity School, took part in peaceable demonstrations aimed at having lunch counters opened to Negroes as well as whites, he was dismissed from the university not long before the date of his graduation, and the entire Divinity School was almost disrupted in the ensuing uproar.

Since mankind is a family the members of it ought to be able to dwell together. The United States Supreme Court has ruled that restrictive covenants are unconstitutional. Nevertheless, we realize that occurrences which are only too frequent are reflected in the play *A Raisin in the Sun*. Here a representative of the Cliburne Park Improvement Society calls upon Negroes who have just purchased a modest residence in Cliburne Park with a very strong effort to buy them off from coming there. In the Southwood district of South San Francisco a few years ago, Mr. Sing Sheng, a former Chinese Nationalist intelligence officer, and his pretty wife and small son, were told by a vote of 174 to 28 that they were not wanted as neighbors. The putting of the matter to the ballot was suggested by Mr. Sheng himself after he received numerous objections to his purchase of a house in the neighborhood. "I didn't know about any race prejudice at all until I came to Southwood," he explained. "I was sure everybody really believed in democracy, so I thought up this vote as a test." When the result of the secret ballot was announced to him, he said: "We'll have to sell the furniture we bought and go somewhere else to live. I hope you people will be happy in your community and that your property values will increase every day."

Since mankind is a family we ought to be able to study together. In certain parts of the United States the plan was, for a long time, that the schools for Negroes and whites should be equal but separate. Finally the Supreme Court ruled that equal but separate is not equal. This seems to be an honest statement of fact, for a few years ago in the six or seven states where there were 1,125,000 Negro children, educational expenditure for the Negro children was $7.50 per child as against $75 per child for the nation. At the time when attempts to set this matter right were leading to terrible violence in Little Rock, Arkansas, a small girl had an idea. It happens that she is blind, so her idea was written out in Braille, then translated by her teacher and sent to the President of the United States. "If I were the President," wrote Leah Russell, twelve years of age, "I would have all of the children blindfolded and send them to school. I would also blindfold the colored children and send them to school, too. I think they would have a lot of fun together, and there wouldn't be any fights." After an address in which I read this letter, someone said to me with much justice that it is more probably the parents of the children who need the blindfolds. Nevertheless, Mr. Eisenhower wrote back to the little girl's teacher: "Thank you for sending me the little essay that Leah Russell was prompted to write as result of the Little Rock difficulties. I hope you will tell her for me that at the age of twelve she has already grasped one of the great moral principles by which we all should live."

Since mankind is one family, its members ought to be able to work together. Twenty years ago racial discrimination was common in employment, and Dr. Mordecai Johnson, head of Howard University, said: "My people are more discouraged now than they have been since they were emancipated from slavery." In the intervening time, however, what James P. Mitchell, former Secretary of Labor, has called "genuinely significant" progress has been made in closing the economic gap between Negro and white citizens. Reporting a Labor Department study in 1960, Mitchell stated that in the past twenty years average earnings of nonwhite men have risen from 41 per cent of those of white workers to 58 per cent, and over the same period the percentage of Negroes in professional and skilled work has doubled. Yet the median income of nonwhite males in 1958 was $2652 compared with $4569 for white males, and the Negro unemployment rate remained disproportionately high.

Family members ought to be able to play together. Therefore, it was an important day when, a few years ago, Althea Gibson won the famous Wimbledon Tennis Singles Championship for women, for she is a Negro girl whose father was hard pressed to purchase her first $18 racket and was unable to take time off from work to meet her at the airport when she came back from Wimbledon. When Althea's picture was taken with the Queen of England, a sports columnist, Bill Leiser, wrote in the San Francisco *Chronicle*:

> In sports equality, and equality of opportunity, are not elements of sermons, lectures, and propaganda. If a man who is yellow, another who is black, and a third who is white take positions at the starting line of the 100 yard dash, the man who reaches the finish line first wins, and nobody knows his color. It has always been the same in boxing in which Negro champions have often outnumbered those of other races. Since the great Branch Rickey determined to (and did) break the color line, with Jackie Robinson, in baseball, this great sport too has been one of equal opportunity to all. A few sports are lagging, we'll admit, but it is still refreshing to see that in this "high society" game of tennis the Queen of England will welcome a little girl from Harlem at, of all exclusive arenas, those of historic Wimbledon, itself.

Since mankind is one family, the members of the family ought to be able to worship together. Yet once upon a time, because he was an Asian, Mahatma Gandhi was denied admission to a Christian church to hear his friend C. F. Andrews preach, so he stood patiently outside the door and listened from there. In the city in which are located the national headquarters of the denomination to which the present writer belongs, less than ten years ago the federation of churches included in a religious survey questionnaire an interrogation concerning the acceptance or non-acceptance of persons of other races as visitors at church services. Out of 118 churches which returned the questionnaire, 23 Protestant churches with white congregations said that they would not accept as visitors at their services members of other races, while 41 more either failed to answer the question or made an ambiguous reply. Of the 54 churches which indicated that they would accept other races, 19 were Negro churches. Such was the state of affairs as reported by the Indianapolis Church Federation in 1952. It would seem that precisely here, in the churches themselves, is the place where first of all the implications of Genesis 10 need to be considered.

7 THE TOWER OF BABEL

(*Genesis* 11:1-9)

The account of the tower of Babel, found in Genesis 11:1-9, gives a historically accurate reflection of the rise of civilization. In earlier chapters we have seen that the general theater of events was the Middle East. Now Genesis 11:2 states, in the King James Version: "And it came to pass, as they journeyed from the east, that they found a plain in the land of Shinar"; or as Moffatt gives the meaning: "there was a migration from the east, and men came upon a plain in the land of Shinar." This tells us that people came from the east into Lower Mesopotamia. According to present knowledge, the first great people in Lower Mesopotamia, who attained to a high civilization and left us a written literature to tell about it, were the Sumerians. The Sumerians were probably there by at least the early fourth millennium B.C. By their own traditions they must have come in from the east, for fondly if dimly they remembered a wonderful land which they called Dilmun and described as "the place where the sun rises." As seen from Lower Mesopotamia, "the place where the sun rises" could be in southwestern Iran. Coming from that area in general, the people we know as the Sumerians may have stopped on the way on the island of Bahrein in the Persian Gulf,

74

and there are some who think that this island itself should be identified with Dilmun. On the northern end of Bahrein Island there are a thousand burial mounds, in which Danish archeologists have recently excavated. They found seals, one unfinished and accordingly manufactured right there, such as some known also in Mesopotamia. This evidence strengthens the belief that the Sumerians did in fact come into Lower Mesopotamia from the east.

That Genesis 11:2 indicates not only a migration from the east but also a coming specifically to Lower Mesopotamia is seen from a consideration of the word "Shinar." This is the Hebrew name for this region, and it is used seven times in the Old Testament. Here it is where men built the tower of Babel, and we will see that that was at Babylon in Lower Mesopotamia. Later, in Daniel 1:2, it is the land to which Nebuchadnezzar carried off the temple treasures he had captured in Palestine, and we know that Nebuchadnezzar was king in Babylon.

Next, we note that Genesis 11:2 states that the people "dwelt" or "settled" in the land of Shinar. This points to the way civilization arose in the ancient Near East and in Mesopotamia. For civilization to arise it was necessary for man to settle down from what we may presume ·was his earlier stage of nomadic existence, and to establish permanent habitation. For the early establishment of such permanent habitation there is evidence now at many sites in the Fertile Crescent, as we call that curving sweep of good land that runs up the valley of the Tigris and Euphrates and down through Syria and Palestine. According to the present assessment of available data, such settlements go back into the fifth millennium B.C. and, at Jericho, even into the seventh. But it was the settlements in Lower Mesopotamia which, although not the first to be made, were maintained in such continuity and with such a development of the arts that we may speak of them as leading to the first truly great civilization. By 3500 B.C. the

Sumerians had developed picture marks on their cylinder seals
into the world's first writing, and were preparing to give us the
world's oldest literature, now known from tens of thousands of
cuneiform tablets from later centuries. By 2500 B.C. they had
developed the skilled craftsmanship represented, for a single
example, by the superb golden vessels of the "royal" cemetery at
Ur, than which nothing finer has ever been made.

But was the civilization in the Near East in fact the earliest
civilization in the whole world? To the best of our knowledge it
was. Compare with the dates we have just given, those for the
earliest known centers of civilization elsewhere in the world. In
India, Mohenjo-daro and the Indus civilization go back to around
2500 B.C. In China, the Great City Shang dates around 1500 B.C.
In Central and South America the dates are later still. W. F.
Albright writes: "Archaeological research has . . . established
beyond doubt that there is no focus of civilization in the earth
that can begin to compete in antiquity and activity with the basin
of the Eastern Mediterranean and the region immediately to the
east of it—Breasted's Fertile Crescent."[1]

As we have seen, however, Genesis 11:2 focuses its account of
early civilization not only in the Near East in general but in Lower
Mesopotamia in particular. How does Mesopotamia compare with
Egypt? According to present knowledge, in its rise civilization in
Egypt was almost contemporary with, but at least partly
dependent upon, civilization in Mesopotamia. It is around 3000
B.C. that the Egyptian civilization comes into our view, and at
that time the evidences of influence from Mesopotamia include:
cylinder seals such as those mentioned above; recessed brick
buildings such as found in Mesopotamian architecture; a painting
of a boat of Mesopotamian type; an ivory carving of lions in
Mesopotamian style.

People came into Lower Mesopotamia from the east, and the
world's first great civilization arose there. These two historical

points are reflected accurately in the account we are studying and so, too, is a third point. The civilization just mentioned was characterized by city and tower or, as we would put it, it was an urban civilization with skyscrapers. "Go to," said these people according to Genesis 11:4, or, as we would say, "Come on" (which is how Moffatt translates it), "let us build us a city and a tower." The material they had to work with is described in verse 3. They had brick burned thoroughly, and anyone who has seen the baked bricks of the Mesopotamian excavations knows what a durable building material this was. "And slime had they for mortar." This cohesive material was bitumen, and it is still found at the springs at Hit on the Euphrates 150 miles above Babylon. With these materials they built their city and their tower.

The name of the city which the people built was Babel (Genesis 11:9). As will shortly be explained, this is the Hebrew form of Babylon. Babylon was the most famous city of Lower Mesopotamia and probably indeed of the entire ancient East. As such, this city is seen in the present account as the epitome and climax of the effort toward civilization. And this city must in fact have been founded by the Sumerians. At present the oldest known inscription to mention Babylon is a text of King Shargalisharri who ruled around 2200 B.C. Although he was an Akkadian, he gave the name of the city in its Sumerian form, thus attesting a Sumerian origin as we have indicated. In Sumerian, the city's name was Ka-dingir, which means "gate of god." When the name was translated into the Semitic language of the Akkadians, it became Bab-ilu, likewise meaning "gate of god." Hebrew is also a Semitic language, and in Hebrew the name was reproduced very similarly as Babel, which is the form in which we find it in Genesis 11:9. In later texts of the New Babylonian period (seventh century B.C. and following) it is found in the form Bab-ilani or "gate of the gods," and it is from this that the Greek form of the name was derived which is reproduced almost exactly in the English Babylon.[2]

As for the tower, it may be said that a tower was the most characteristic form of architectural construction in ancient Mesopotamia. Not just any tower is meant, but a particular kind of tower which we know as a "ziggurat." This name comes from a word in the Akkadian language which means "to be high or raised up." Such a tower was raised in successive terraces high above the Mesopotamian plain, had a shrine on top, and was accordingly a form of temple. The ruins of more than two dozen such temple towers have been found in Mesopotamia. Including ziggurats attested by drawings and inscriptions, André Parrot has made a list of thirty-three such structures in twenty-seven different cities.[3]

The building of such towers was certainly done as early as the Sumerian period. At Ur the oldest ziggurat may have been constructed by Mes-Anne-Pada, founder of the First Dynasty, to which period belongs the "royal" cemetery mentioned above. Then in the Third Dynasty, around 2000 B.C., a much larger ziggurat was built over the first one. This was done by King Ur-Nammu, whose name and title are still to be read on the bricks of the monument. In the sixth century B.C. Nabonidus of Babylon repaired the upper part of the structure but, in an inscription, gave credit to Ur-Nammu as the former builder. Nabonidus also said that Ur-Nammu did not complete the work, but that it was finished by his son Shulgi. This tower, although now in ruins of course, is still the best preserved of all these monuments and gives a powerful impression to the visitor who sees it loom up above the Mesopotamian plain. The base was 200 feet by 150 feet, the core was of unbaked brick, and the facing, about eight feet thick, was of baked brick set in bitumen.

As for the ziggurat at Babylon, most of its bricks have long since been carried away for other buildings, and where it once stood there is scarcely more than an enormous hole filled with water which has seeped in from the Euphrates. Nevertheless, the excavator of Babylon, Robert Koldewey, was able to obtain some architectural evidence, and there is also some information in cuneiform sources and in Herodotus. The name of the tower was E-temen-an-ki, meaning "house of the foundation of heaven and earth." It stood in a very large enclosure about 1500 feet square. It was erected upon a square foundation, each side of which was about 300 feet long. The interior was of dried brick and the outer shell, almost 50 feet thick, of baked brick. From a cuneiform tablet and from Herodotus it is gathered that the tower rose in seven stories to a height of almost 300 feet, and thus it was second only to the great pyramids of Egypt in imposing mass. Under the later kings Nabopolassar and Nebuchadnezzar, the structure attained its greatest magnificence, and the temple on top was covered with blue enameled tile. How early the tower originated is not known, but in its very impressive character it must have represented to all who knew Mesopotamia the very high point of man's striving toward civilization.

These, then, are historically accurate allusions to the rise of civilization contained in the story of the tower of Babel. People came into Lower Mesopotamia from the east, they settled there and built the world's first great, flourishing civilization, and this civilization was characterized by a great city and especially by a great tower.

Next, the tower of Babel narrative gives a psychologically accurate indication of certain problems of civilization. Let us say at once that civilization is a very valuable achievement. Doubtless, only one who has tried to get along without it can properly appreciate how much it means to us, the beneficiaries of all that has been developed across the thousands of years. This, at any rate, was the experience of Bud Boyd, outdoor writer for the San Francisco *Chronicle*, who, in the summer of 1960, enacted the role of "the last man on earth." With his wife and three children, aged fifteen, twelve, and eight, he went into a remote mountain wilderness, taking only what the hypothetical survivor of The Bomb might hope to pick up hastily and carry with him: an ax, a pocketknife, a rope, twine, and salt. To try to live with only this equipment in a mountain wilderness turned out to be, according to the published newspaper reports, extremely difficult, and anyone who has tried to live in similar surroundings with even much more equipment can readily believe that this was the case. The elements were bigger and more formidable than man: cold, exhaustion, and hunger soon threatened, and the fight for survival became terrifying. Ending his first report, Boyd wrote: "Our fire pushes at the black night and it is the only light in our world. We are all alone. Scared to death." Suddenly it seemed as if one of the greatest things man had ever accomplished was just to get himself up off the ground and have a bed, a chair, and a table. Now they were back on the ground. "We have lived our lifetimes on our feet. Now we are living on the ground. To sleep, we lie down in the dirt. To eat, we squat crosslegged. We must crawl to enter our shelter. We squat before the fireplace to cook or eat. In all, these have been the most brutish, most miserable days of our lives." As for a supermarket, or electric switch, or water faucet, these were incredible wonders. "It set us all to thinking," wrote Boyd. "For the first time in our lives we could feel a kinship with some unknown, forgotten ancestor who lived in a cave. He sat beside a fire, just as we were doing. He had a scrap of skin for clothing, and he lived on what he killed with a stone, or grubbed with his hands. Now, we know the utter misery of his existence. As we sat by the fire last night we realized the thousands of tiny, tottering, tortuous steps man has taken upward."

Yes, civilization is a great and valuable thing, and we have every reason to be grateful to those ancient Mesopotamian peoples who took so many of the steps up the road for us. Nevertheless, civilization brings with it its own peculiar problems, and some of these are pointed to very acutely by the story of the tower of Babel. One is pride. "Let us make us a name," said the people in Genesis 11:4. Their desire was to make themselves famous, to make themselves a reputation, to secure their name against oblivion. Driver says that theirs was a work of "misdirected ambition," and Skinner speaks of the "restless, scheming, soaring human mind" which is revealed in the story. In his book *Beyond Tragedy* Reinhold Niebuhr discusses the tower of Babel, and points out that inevitable and inescapable pride is involved in every human enterprise. His illustrations include the building of the Egyptian pyramids by the kings of Egypt who wished to assure immortality for themselves, but whose work accentuated the injustices of slavery in Egypt and thus accelerated the very decay which the pyramids were intended to defy; and the completion of the League of Nations building in Geneva just in time to hear the plea of the emperor of Ethiopia for a justice which the League was unable to grant, a failure which brought the League to its final ruin. So Niebuhr concludes: "Every form of human culture, whether religious, rational or scientific, is subject to the same corruption, because all are products of the same human heart, which tries to deny its finite limitations."[4]

Materialism is another problem characteristic of civilization. To build a very large and massive tower seemed to the people of Babylon the most important thing of all to do. In his book on *The Crisis of Our Age* Pitirim A. Sorokin describes ours as a sensate culture. By that he means that it is based on the belief that true reality and true value are mainly or exclusively sensory. That which is sensory is that which we can see, hear, taste, touch, or smell. This belief in that which is sensory Sorokin calls the root of the tree of our culture, a tree which has brought forth both splendid and poisonous fruit. Positive fruit includes unprecedented development of natural sciences and technological inventions. Poisonous fruit includes fatal narrowing of the realm of true reality and true value. Anything beyond the senses is doubtful as reality or fictitious as value. Excluded, therefore, are revelation, mysticism, and faith. But with such exclusions man is degraded, values are atomized, and culture is allowed to disintegrate. To this diagnosis Sorokin adds the prognosis:

> As in the declining stage of the Greco-Roman sensate culture, the aridity of thought and sterility of creativeness will increasingly pervade the whole sensate supersystem until Western society awakens to all the hollowness of its streamlined culture. Confronted with this dead shell of what before was a magnificent creation, it will have but one exit from the situation: to leave the hollow corpse for something that lives and creates, for an ideational or idealistic or integral form of culture.[5]

Self-deification is a further problem. The builders of the tower of Babel thought of it as a structure "whose top may reach unto heaven" (Genesis 11:4). By erecting a tower of such height man might make himself equal with God, and if man is equal with God then God is unnecessary and man has himself come into the position of God. That such a bold self-deification is, upon occasion, undertaken by man we know well enough in our own time. The League of Fighting Godless in Russia, for example, once appealed to a certain portion of the labor movement with these words:

> The Stakhanov movement must play an outstanding role in the overthrow of religion. It signifies a mighty increase in the power of man, who is conquering nature and breaking down all previously imposed standards. If the scholars of the bourgeois world maintain that there are limits beyond which man's perception and man's strength cannot go, that there are matters which a limited intelligence will not perceive, it is evident that under the proletarian deliverance from religion the creation of conscious workers in a classless society can, with the aid of the latest technical acquisitions, proceed to tasks which man, fettered by re-

ligion, would never have dared to face. In a socialist society knowledge is free from narrow limits. There is no bulwark which bolshevists cannot take by storm.[6]

These are problems in civilization, acute problems in our own time, to which the ancient story of Babel acutely points. But once more, this story which gives a historically accurate reflection of the rise of civilization, and a psychologically penetrating indication of the problems of civilization, gives also a theologically correct description of God's judgment on civilization. The most important point in what is set forth in this regard may well consist in the fact that God sees what man does. "The Lord came down to see the city and the tower, which the children of men builded" (Genesis 11:5). Man may go forward on his arrogant way, but he is still under the surveillance of the Almighty. And the Lord who sees may also act in judgment upon that which affronts him. Here, God confounded the language of the people and scattered them abroad. The report of this event is connected in our story with the name of the city. In the Hebrew of Genesis 11:9 there is a play on words which may be reproduced approximately by rendering in English, as the American Translation does: "That was why its name was called Babel, because it was there that the Lord made a babble of the language of the whole earth." The confounding of language seems to symbolize the fact that when men exalt themselves against God they are up against something greater than themselves and they are cast down and rendered unable even to understand one another. Walter Russell Bowie brings out the symbolism in this way: "Differences of language are a source of trouble, the symbol and accentuation of division, strangeness, suspicions, and hostility. And by profound insight, again, this fact was linked with the overweening spirit by which men are always trying to make themselves bigger than they are."[7]

As it reveals to man, especially to civilized man, the danger of his pride, the Bible story of the tower of Babel points man to the true and humble worship of the God who always sees him exactly as he is. Out of such true and humble worship, man may once again find it possible to communicate better with his fellow man. In fact the Bible which, in this story, tells of the confusion of human tongues, is at the same time the book which, through translation already—at least in part—into more than one thousand languages, is providing the most nearly universal medium of communication among men.

8   ABRAHAM: MAN OF FAITH
(*Genesis* 11:10-17:27)

The first part of the book of Genesis, with which we have been dealing, has to do with early events. In the accounts which extend from creation through the tower of Babel, we have seen how man was made as a creature of God, how he climbed to civilization, and how he fell in character as he became proud and rebellious. The second part of the book, beginning at Genesis 11:10, tells of the patriarchs. God's work with men now focuses upon one particular group. After the flood, as we have already seen, the earth was inhabited and populated by the descendants of Noah. Noah's three sons, Shem, Ham, and Japheth, were the eponymous ancestors of the Semitic, Hamitic, and Japhitic or, as we would say, Indo-European, peoples. Among the three sons, attention is now directed to Shem, that is, to the Semitic people; and among the progeny of Shem, to the line that leads to Abraham and his descendants, that is, to the Israelite people. This is the line we start down at Genesis 11:10: Shem, Arpachshad, Shelah, Eber, Peleg, Reu, Serug, Nahor, Terah, and Abram or, in the variant form of his name, Abraham. Abraham's descendants, in turn, were Isaac, Jacob, and Jacob's twelve sons. The persons of the last group were recognized as the "patriarchs" of the Israelite people or, as we might say, the "founding fathers." Hebrews 7:4 speaks of "Abraham the patriarch," and Acts 7:8 says that Abraham became the father of Isaac, Isaac of Jacob, "and Jacob of the twelve patriarchs." Therefore, the title applies to the men from Abraham through the twelve sons of Jacob. It is with the patriarchs and especially with Abraham that we are presently concerned.

What kind of records do we have concerning Abraham and the patriarchs? We have recognized that in the first part of Genesis we have been dealing with accounts to which the terms "myth" and "legend," in the technical sense of those designations, may be applied. To put the matter in our own words, we have said that the account of creation is a sublime poem in which the language of man's activity is used to describe that which goes beyond the capacity of man's language to describe, namely, the activity of God himself in his creative work; and that the accounts of Adam and Noah and the rest are poetic narratives in which dim remembrances of mankind's early experiences are vividly presented in order to elevate, to inspire, and to move the hearer or reader. Now at the point of Abraham and the patriarchs, are we still in the realm of legend? That this is the case was affirmed by Julius Wellhausen in an opinion expressed more than eighty years ago and echoed frequently by many other scholars ever since. In 1878 Wellhausen published the first volume of his *History of Israel* which was issued in English translation in 1885 as *Prolegomena to the History of Israel*. In this work he spoke repeatedly of "the patriarchal legend," and said that in this legend "we attain to no historical knowledge of the patriarchs, but only of the time when the stories about them arose in the Israelite people; this later age is here unconsciously projected, in its inner and its outward features, into hoar antiquity, and is reflected there like a glorified mirage."[1] The stories about the patriarchs arose, Wellhausen held, in Middle and North Israel, where they were written down in the two forms of the "J" and the "E" documents, to which it is customary to ascribe dates around 850 and 750 B.C. respectively. Still later in the exile, the stories continued to be worked on and were put in the form in which they are found in the "P" document, around 500 B.C. So the documents purport to tell about events one thousand to fifteen hundred years earlier, but they really reflect the circumstances in Israel and in the exile in the time of their own composition, from the ninth to the fifth centuries. As for Abraham himself, Wellhausen found the figure of the first patriarch "somewhat difficult to interpret." Abraham was of course not to be regarded as a historical person; with more likelihood he might be considered as "a free creation of unconscious art." Along with Isaac and Jacob, he was an ideal prototype of the true Israelite.[2]

It is obvious that the opinion just described derives its chief support from the supposed fact that the patriarchal narratives reflect the conditions of a relatively late time and do not correspond with the time in which the patriarchs are said to have lived. The period in which the patriarchs are represented as having lived may be ascertained by adding up the relevant chronological notations in the Old Testament documents. When this is done on the basis of the Hebrew text, it leads to a date somewhat before 1900 B.C. for Abraham. According to Archbishop James Ussher, whose chronology was taken into the margin of the King James Version of the Bible, the birth of Abraham was in 1996 B.C., and his entry into Canaan seventy-five years later (Genesis 12:4) was therefore in 1921 B.C. In the Greek translation known as the Septuagint, however, there is a difference of two hundred and fifteen years and Abraham's entry into Canaan would fall about 1700 B.C. The really important question would seem to be, therefore, not whether the several documents were compiled at the time to which critical opinion commonly ascribes them, but whether they preserve actual historical information from the earlier times about which they tell. And the way to form at least a reasonable judgment on this matter would seem to be to compare what is told with what is otherwise known about the times in question. There are now more materials available for such a comparison than was formerly the case. From archeology considerable information is available about the Near East in the time in which the Old Testament pictures Abraham and the patriarchs as having lived, as well as about the later centuries in which the documents may have been put into their final form. On the basis of this information it seems to the present writer correct to say that the accounts in question do not reflect the conditions of the ninth to fifth centuries in which Wellhausen thought the "patriarchal legend" arose, but that they do fit the conditions of the twentieth to seventeenth centuries B.C., which is the time within which, on either chronology given above, the patriarchal narratives would fall. This may now be illustrated with some examples relating particularly to Abraham.

Places mentioned in the narrative concerning Abraham were actually in existence at that time. Ur of the Chaldees (Genesis 11:31), a site in the Lower Mesopotamian region which later belonged to the Chaldeans, must have been settled around 4000 B.C. as stone implements and hand-painted pottery show, and by 2500 B.C., still long before Abraham, its "royal" cemetery contained jewelry and gold vessels as fine as anything in the world. Haran (Genesis 11:31) in Upper Mesopotamia is a known place in ancient Near Eastern history, and still exists as a Muslim village where the inhabitants revere Abraham as an Islamic saint. Shechem (Genesis 12:6) and Bethel (Genesis 12:8) are excavated sites in Palestine and were in existence in the time of Abraham. The South (Genesis 12:9 KJV and ASV) or the Negeb (RSV) is the southern part of Judah and familiar from the international news of our time.

Concerning the Negeb we may speak in somewhat more detail,

since it is less familiar and since the archeological situation there has a bearing on a decision between the two alternate dates given above for Abraham. As reported in his book *Rivers in the Desert, A History of the Negev*, Nelson Glueck has explored this region archeologically at four hundred sites. He finds that there was a settled civilization in the Negeb in the period known as Middle Bronze I, the twenty-first to the nineteenth centuries B.C., with nomadism ensuing again from the eighteenth to the eleventh centuries.[3] If, as one of the dates given above would indicate, Abraham came to Palestine prior to 1900 B.C., he would have been in the Negeb in Middle Bronze I, and Glueck calls this the Abrahamitic period and suggests our picturing Abraham as journeying there at that time, "not through an empty country, but one dotted with developed villages and towns."[4] While it is true that the biblical narrative describes Abraham not only as journeying (Genesis 12:9; 13:1, 3) but also as dwelling (Genesis 20:1; 24:62) in the Negeb, the word "dwell" is used also otherwise (Genesis 13:12) of Abraham and of Lot in their tents, and could surely represent a type of nomadic or seminomadic existence which would have been thoroughly possible even in the ensuing nomadic period in the Negeb. If we take the second date given above for Abraham, namely, around 1700 B.C., we must in fact place him in this later period and specifically in what is designated as Middle Bronze II, the nineteenth to the sixteenth centuries B.C. Now in Genesis 20:1, Abraham is described not only as dwelling in the Negeb but also as sojourning in Gerar. The word "sojourn," which is used also of Abraham's stay in Egypt (Genesis 12:10), contains the word *ger* or "foreigner," and really means that he lived there as a foreigner. Gerar itself must have been a city of importance in the time of Abraham, since it is described as under a king named Abimelech (Genesis 20:2). He in turn is called king of the Philistines (Genesis 21:32; 26:1, 8), but that is a simple anachronism owing to the fact that Gerar

lay in a region that was later occupied by the Philistines. Since
the later occupation of the Philistines was in the southern coastal
plain and the western Negeb, we are pointed to that area if we
search for ancient Gerar. The site has in fact now been found
with much probability at a large mound, Tell Abu Hureira, on
the edge of the Wadi esh-Shari'ah, between Beer-sheba and Gaza.
As thus located, Gerar was on the border of the permanently
settled country to the north and near to the pasture lands of the
nomads to the south. It was a likely place for Abraham, with his
flocks and herds (Genesis 13:2, 5), to live. For our purpose, the
important point is to establish whether this place, mentioned in
the Bible in connection with Abraham, was actually in existence
in the time in which the Bible pictures Abraham as living, and
once again the answer turns out to be in the affirmative. In the
exploration of Tell Abu Hureira, sherds were found dating from
every phase of the Bronze Age, and, assuming the highly probable
identification with Gerar, this shows that Gerar was a settled
place within the whole period in which, on any reckoning, the
time of Abraham must fall. But the sherds were especially abun-
dant from Middle Bronze II (nineteenth to sixteenth centuries
B.C.) at which time the city evidently flourished particularly. As
the city of King Abimelech, Gerar was evidently a very important
place at the time of Abraham. Accordingly, we would be inclined
to place Abraham in Middle Bronze II, and this is precisely where
the second date given for him above, around 1700 B.C., would
put him. In fact Y. Aharoni, whose detailed discussion of Gerar
has been followed in the sketch above, speaks unhesitatingly of
Middle Bronze II as the age of the patriarchs.[5] While we have
now diverged from Nelson Glueck's date for Abraham in Middle
Bronze I (corresponding to our first alternate date given above
of prior to 1900 B.C.), and accepted as the more probable a date
in Middle Bronze II (corresponding to our second alternate of
around 1700 B.C.), we are still in full agreement with Glueck

when he speaks of "the Bible's almost incredibly correct historical memory," and says that "no archaeological discovery has ever controverted a Biblical reference."[6]

Proceeding now to another test of the narrative against the period it is supposed to represent, it can be said that names used in the account about Abraham are those of the time. Abram and Abraham appear to be variant forms of one name, and still another variant, Abamram, is found slightly later at Babylon. Abraham's brother was Nahor, and in the Mari tablets around 1700 B.C. a city of Nakhur, near Haran, is mentioned. Abraham's grandson was Jacob, and in the form Ya'qob-el this name is found in an eighteenth-century text from Chagar Bazar.

Laws and customs presupposed in the narrative are also known now from ancient Near Eastern texts. Hurrian texts of the fifteenth century found at Nuzi in northern Mesopotamia reveal legal regulations which had doubtless prevailed for centuries. A man and wife who had no child might adopt a slave who would serve them as long as they lived and then inherit their estate when they died. But if a real son was born in the meantime, the adopted son would have to give place to him. This could be why when Abraham had no son of his own he anticipated that his slave Eliezer would be his heir, and why when a son of his own was promised it was said about Eliezer: "This man shall not be your heir; your own son shall be your heir" (Genesis 15:4). Some of the marriage contracts at Nuzi stipulated that if a wife did not bear any children for her husband, she should provide him with a handmaid to bear children for him. This is what Sarai did when she gave her maid, Hagar the Egyptian, to Abraham. Nuzi law also stipulated that if the slave wife bore a child, she and the child should not be driven out, and this could provide the legal basis for Abraham's apprehension when Sarai, having at last had a son of her own, demanded that Abraham expel Hagar and Ishmael. Hittite laws of the fourteenth

century have also been found at Boghazköy, which likewise
doubtless reach much farther back, and are of interest here because Abraham dealt with Hittites at Hebron when he purchased
for a burial place the cave of the field of Machpelah. In a real-
estate transaction, Hittite law specified that if an entire property
was purchased, the buyer became liable to the ruler for certain
services, for which he was not liable if he purchased only a small
part of the property. This could explain why Abraham tried
(Genesis 23:9) to buy only the cave at the end of the field, but
Ephron insisted (Genesis 23:11) on selling cave and field together. Hittite legal documents also list the exact number of trees
in a real-estate sale, and this may explain why "all the trees that
were in the field" are explicitly mentioned in the description of
the contract in Genesis 23:17.

The political situation may also be noted both in general and
in particular. In general, Abraham is able to wander freely from
Mesopotamia to Palestine to Egypt and back again to Palestine.
In many later periods this would not have been possible, but
the Mari texts of the eighteenth century likewise show that there
was then free travel over the entire Fertile Crescent, while according to the nineteenth-century Execration Texts from Egypt,
Palestine was at that time held only loosely or not at all by Egypt,
which accords with the fact that afterward in Palestine Abraham
encounters no Egyptian rulers. In connection with Abraham's
visit to Egypt, a tomb painting at Beni Hasan, halfway between
Cairo and Luxor, is of interest. Dated about 1892 B.C., it shows
thirty-seven Asians who have come down to Egypt. They proceed
on foot. Their children and goods are on donkeys. They wear
many-colored garments. The men have black beards. The women's
hair is bound with circlets and hangs down their backs. Save for
the fact that the leader's name is given as Ibsha, and that the
date is somewhat earlier than that which we have now preferred
for Abraham, it could almost be a picture of the patriarch and
some of his people.

In particular, Genesis 14, provides detailed references to the international situation contemporary with Abraham. Here four kings from elsewhere come and fight with the five kings of five cities in the Dead Sea valley, and Abraham is involved because he has to rescue his nephew Lot, whom they take captive. The identification of the four kings has proved difficult, but a recent study[7] has suggested the following as a possible solution. Chedor-laomer king of Elam could be Kudur-Lagamara which is a good Elamite name. From Elam a king could come to Palestine only across and in co-operation with Babylonia, and this explains the appearance of Amraphel king of Shinar, for we have already seen that Shinar is Lower Mesopotamia or Babylonia. The -el on the end of this king's name could be the Semitic word for "god," representing the deification of the king, and Amraph-could be a form of the name Hammurabi. Arioch king of Ellasar, in turn, has a good Hurrite name, and Tidal king of Goiim can be recognized as the Hittite royal name Tudhaliyas. In the time of the Mari tablets, the Hittite capital of Hattusa, the ruins of which are at Boghazköy, fell to outside conquerors and Tudhaliyas, as one of the foreign rulers, was indeed a king "of Goiim," for that means a king "of the foreigners." As for Hammurabi, he could have moved into Palestine only after he took Mari, the rival city above him in the Mesopotamian valley, which he did in the thirty-second year of his reign. Since the dates of Hammurabi's reign are probably 1728-1686 B.C., this means that he would have been in Palestine (presumably on a campaign the larger objective of which was against Egypt) somewhat after 1700 B.C., and this is in agreement with the date which we have preferred above for Abraham.

The foregoing are at least some examples of the kind of evidence we find when we try to study the records concerning Abraham and his immediate successors against the background of their time as now known from archeology. As far as the present writer can see, there is no convincing reason not to accept the substantial historicity of the accounts and to deal with Abraham and the other patriarchs as real persons. This is the way the matter now looks to others, too. For example, in 1959, eighty-one years after Wellhausen's *History of Israel,* John Bright published *A History of Israel* and began it with a full chapter on The Patriarchs. He writes: "As the early second millennium has emerged into the light of day, it has become clear that the patriarchal narratives, far from reflecting the circumstances of a later day, fit precisely in the age of which they purport to tell."[8] He also acknowledges, as we must, that the evidence of archeology is indirect and does not prove the patriarchal stories true in detail, but he says flatly, in a way much like the quotation from Nelson Glueck given above, that "no evidence has come to light contradicting any item in the tradition,"[9] and with this conclusion we can also express full agreement.

What kind of a person was Abraham? According to the Bible record he was a man of faith. Here, too, our picture of Abraham is different from what it used to be. Along with the belief that the Bible account in general was a "mirage" "projected . . . into hoar antiquity," went usually the conviction that the Bible record of Abraham's religion in particular was an anachronism. To say that God made a promise to Abraham and a covenant with him, seemed like reading back into an early time what could only have been a late idea. Surely back in Abraham's ancient time about all there was by way of religion was animism and polydaemonism, that is, belief in many spirits and demons. Actually this supposition would apply to some of the Arabs before Muhammad, concerning whom Wellhausen gathered information,[10] but it would not describe even the major nonbiblical religions of the Near East in the second millennium B.C. These, while they recognized many deities, were already highly developed and organized, and at least directed man reverently toward the great powers of nature. Furthermore, covenant forms, at least in human relations, are found in Sumerian texts of the third millennium B.C., and it seems likely that covenant ideas spread from Mesopotamian sources to many peoples in the second millennium B.C.[11]

Actually of course the Bible itself explicitly states that the ancestors of Israel before Abraham were polytheists, for it is said in Joshua 24:2: "Your fathers lived of old beyond the Euphrates, Terah, the father of Abraham and of Nahor; and they served other gods"; and we know that the two places of Terah's residence, Ur and Haran, were centers of the moon cult. Yet between Adam and Abraham there may have been ancestors who knew the true God, for it is said of Seth, that "at that time men began to call upon the name of the Lord" (Genesis 4:26); of Enoch, that he "walked with God" (Genesis 5:22); and of Noah, that God made a covenant with him (Genesis 9:8 f.). As for Abraham, he may well have done independent thinking for himself, and he is certainly pictured in the records as having received revelations from God: the Lord appeared to him (Genesis 12:7; 17:1; 18:1); the word of the Lord came to him in a vision (Genesis 15:1); and God spoke to him (Genesis 22:1). As a result, Abraham knew God as the "most high" (Genesis 14:22), the "almighty" (Genesis 17:1), the "everlasting" (Genesis 21:33), and "the God of heaven and of the earth" (Genesis 24:3).

In the faith of Abraham, certain aspects stand out particularly. His was a personal faith. How personal it was, may appear in the fact that he put the name of God in the common Semitic form *el* into the name of his first offspring in the sense of a prayer: the name of Ishmael, son of Hagar the Egyptian, means "May God hear." Afterward the God of Abraham was called exactly that—the God of Abraham. To Abraham's son Isaac the deity said: "I am the God of Abraham your father" (Genesis 26:24); to Abraham's grandson Jacob he said: "I am the Lord, the God of Abraham your father [meaning, as we would say more literally, your grandfather] and the God of Isaac" (Genesis

28:13). Much later still, Moses was told to say to the Israelites: "The God of your fathers, the God of Abraham, the God of Isaac, and the God of Jacob, has sent me to you" (Exodus 3:15). There was evidently a personal relationship between Abraham and his God, and this was renewed again and again in the cases of Isaac and of Jacob. It is true that the records preserve individual names for the deity as worshiped by each of the three patriarchs: the God of Abraham is "El Shaddai," usually translated as "God Almighty" (Genesis 17:1); the God of Isaac is "the Fear of Isaac" (Genesis 31:42); and the God of Jacob is "the Mighty One of Jacob" (Genesis 49:24). This may look like henotheism, and in concluding his study of the matter Albrecht Alt says that Abraham, Isaac, and Jacob remain in a position back of Moses, but the lines are recognizable which lead from their gods to the God of Israel.[12] On the other hand, W. F. Albright speaks of each patriarch as choosing his God for himself and selecting a "different manifestation" of the God who was later known in Israel.[13] Since the relationship seems to have been passed on from father to son to son, it would seem probable that each man did recognize that his allegiance was to the same God whom his father had served, even though known to himself under some particular aspect or name. At any event, to the God he knew, each man in turn seems to have stood in that kind of personal relationship which was so distinctively characteristic in the case of Abraham.

The faith of Abraham was also a covenant faith. A covenant is an agreement, and God made an agreement with Abraham. It was, however, a remarkable agreement, for in content it consisted exclusively of a promise made by God to Abraham. On the other side, there was only a sign, namely circumcision, which gave a concrete indication that the covenant existed, and identified Abraham and his descendants as the recipients of the covenant.[14] The promise of God is stated already in Genesis 15.

It is a promise to give Abraham land and posterity. Abraham was a seminomad, and there is nothing a wanderer desires more than these things that were thus promised. Then in Genesis 17 the rite of circumcision is given as the sign of the covenant.

The priority of God's promise in the experience of Abraham leads to yet another aspect of the man's faith: it was a trusting faith. The only thing that was really required was for Abraham to trust in God who made the almost unbelievable promise to him. Abraham did actually exercise this believing trust in God, and the fact that he did so was recognized as the outstanding feature in the attitude of Abraham: "And he believed the Lord; and he reckoned it to him as righteousness" (Genesis 15:6).

These aspects of the faith of Abraham are further illustrated by the way in which Abraham is described. Abraham talked with God. The personal nature of his faith is shown by the fact that much of the narrative is in dialogue. God spoke to Abraham and Abraham replied, inquired, pleaded, and conversed with God. Like Enoch before him, Abraham walked with God. This may be taken both literally and figuratively. To obtain the covenant promise Abraham had to walk forth, literally, to the land which he was to have. With his father he went out from Ur of the Chaldees to Haran. To stop there, as they did, was incomplete obedience. After the death of Terah, Abraham went on again, on to the land of Canaan. And in the literal walking, Abraham walked spiritually, too, with the God he knew and trusted. When he was ninety-nine years old, God's word to him was still: "Walk before me and be blameless" (Genesis 17:1). The inner meaning of his going forth is interpreted in its deep significance in Hebrews 11:8-10: "By faith Abraham obeyed when he was called to go out to a place which he was to receive as an inheritance; and he went out, not knowing where he was to go. By faith he sojourned in the land of promise, as in a foreign land, living in tents with Isaac and Jacob, heirs with him of the same promise. For he looked forward to the city which has foundations, whose builder and maker is God." And Abraham was the friend of God. His trust was the mark of his friendship with the God who had befriended him. That Abraham received this title, and the reason why he did, are stated by James 2:23: "Abraham believed God, and it was reckoned to him as righteousness and he was called the friend of God." By the same title—in Arabic, el-Khalil—he is still known throughout the entire Near East.

What kind of an influence, then, has Abraham had in the world? He was so distinctively a man of faith that he has been recognized as the father of the faithful everywhere. The physical descendants of Abraham were always understandably proud of their lineage from him. With reference to such descent they called him their "father," as Paul does in Romans 4:12: "our father Abraham." Like Abraham, they too were circumcised, and by this mark were identified as participants in the same covenant.

But in the same fourth chapter of Romans where Paul as a Jew calls Abraham "our father," he makes as a Christian an acute observation concerning Abraham. He observes that Abraham's faith was reckoned to him as righteousness already before he was circumcised. As even a rabbi who might be disposed to argue the matter on the basis of literal texts would have to admit, it is in Genesis 15 that it is stated that Abraham believed the Lord and he reckoned it to him as righteousness, and only in Genesis 17 that Abraham was given the rite and sign of circumcision. Therefore, Paul draws the logical conclusion, the blessing was upon Abraham in his faith. About Abraham the really important thing was not a physical fact which came later, but a spiritual fact which came first. Therefore, the really important kind of relationship to Abraham is not physical but spiritual. Regardless of physical lineage and the mark in the flesh indicative thereof, the only thing that really matters in being descended from Abraham is having the same kind of faith as he had. This is possible to all, Jews and Gentiles alike, and in this way Abraham is the father of them all, insofar as they are believers. It is a scriptural fact that Abraham's faith was reckoned as righteousness before he was circumcised; it is a logical deduction that "the purpose was to make him the father of all who believe" (Romans 4:11).

9 SODOM AND GOMORRAH: CAN IT HAPPEN NOW? (*Genesis 18-19*)

What happened to Sodom and Gomorrah? Some have felt that no actual happening was involved, that we have here only an imaginary narrative of a sort which is actually quite widespread in the world. T. K. Cheyne writing in 1892,[1] and Hermann Gunkel writing in 1901,[2] collected from Arabia, Greece, and elsewhere various myths or legends which told how a one-time flourishing place was destroyed because of the wickedness of its inhabitants and how perhaps some pious persons were rescued, and they considered the Genesis account to belong to the same class of stories. But, writing soon afterward, S. R. Driver remarked that analogies of that kind, however numerous, "are not in themselves sufficient to show the Biblical narrative to be unhistorical," and himself adopted the view "that the destruction of the four cities [of Genesis, Chapter 14] was a real event, happening in Abraham's time."[3] As we now study the story in its setting, it is hoped to show that the latter conclusion is the probable one, even though the account may very well be admitted to have been often told and long handed down, and to have the vivid and even anthropomorphic touches of the storyteller.

The story, called by Driver "one of the most graphically and finely written narratives in the Old Testament,"[4] unfolds in the following points. First, as we recall from Genesis 12, when Abraham journeyed to Canaan, he took with him Lot, the son of his deceased brother Haran. Second, as is told in Genesis 13, in due time both Abraham and his nephew had numerous flocks and herds, so numerous in fact that the two men could no longer dwell in the same region without friction. The herdsmen of Abraham's cattle and the herdsmen of Lot's cattle began to strive together over the water and grazing land which were insufficient for both. Abraham was a man of peace and desired no such strife. At the time the tents of the two men were pitched between Bethel and Ai. Bethel is twelve miles north of Jerusalem, Ai one and three-quarters miles east of Bethel. The location is on the central watershed, at the head of passes which run east and west through the hills of what we know as Judea. One spot in particular, known as Burj Beitin or Tower of Bethel, offers what George Adam Smith called "one of the great view-points of Palestine."[5] The view extends in all directions, and this may be the very place where Abraham said to Lot: "Is not the whole land before you?" Magnanimously the older man offered the younger his choice, either the left or the right. Facing east in the act of orientation, the left was to the north and comprised the hill country. The right was to the south. Flowing southward, not many miles away but far below, is the Jordan River. Looking from this point, a modern traveler wrote: "To the East there rises in the foreground the jagged range of the hills above Jericho; in the distance the dark wall of Moab; between them lies the wide valley of the Jordan, its course marked by the track of tropical forest growth in which its rushing stream is enveloped."[6] "And Lot lifted up his eyes," it is written, "and beheld all the plain of Jordan" (KJV). The Hebrew word for plain used here is *kikkar* which literally means "round," so we might render the meaning by saying that Lot beheld the whole Circle or Oval of the Jordan. This would probably mean the basin which includes not only the lower course of the river but also the Dead Sea. In geological time when Palestine was first lifted up above the ocean, a great fault or fracture in the earth's crust was formed here. In this fissure a part of the ocean was imprisoned. Long ago, therefore, there was a great inland sea which gradually shrank. Ultimately there remained Lake Huleh in the north, 229 feet above sea level, the Sea of Galilee, 696 feet below sea level, and the Dead Sea, 1290 feet below sea level. When Lot looked down into this profound rift he saw a valley well watered and fertile. It was like the garden of Eden, or like the Nile-watered land of Egypt. Already too, in the Middle Bronze Age, as we know from excavations, it was a well-populated area. This Lot chose. He turned his back on the hill country of the north, rigorous and forbidding, and went down among the cities of the valley and moved his tent as far as Sodom. The area he left behind was the land of promise; the cities of the valley, especially Sodom, were wicked; but that was his choice. Emil G. Kraeling writes: "The son of Abraham's brother thus foolishly relinquished the whole land of Canaan, the promised land in which he might have had a share, to Abraham, and therewith removed himself from the pale of the destiny reserved for that land!"[7]

The third point in the unfolding story is reached when we find, in Genesis 14, that living amidst the cities of the valley, Lot was involved in their political fortunes. Five of the cities evidently formed a sort of confederation. These were Sodom, Gomorrah, Admah, Zeboiim, and Bela or Zoar. These were attacked by four kings from the north in a military campaign, some aspects of which were considered in our preceding chapter about Abraham. Here we note that Lot at this time "dwelt in Sodom" (Genesis 14:12); he has left his tents and become a city man. Therefore, in the victory of the invaders over the cities, Lot and his people fell among the prisoners, but Abraham managed to rescue him.

And so we come to the fourth part of the story, that which is narrated in Genesis 18–19, and that with which we are chiefly concerned. Lot was living in his house in Sodom, sheltered by its roof, and protected by its door. He was presumably still prosperous and he was accustomed to sit, as the prosperous citizens did, "in the gate" (Genesis 19:1) of Sodom. It was a feature of an ancient walled city that at the city gate was a square with benches. Here was a place of business, of the administration of justice, and of endless conversation. Yet Lot is still called a sojourner (19:9) or foreigner, and was evidently not fully accepted as one of the men of Sodom.

Abraham, meanwhile, was dwelling in his tent by the oaks of Mamre. These oak or terebinth trees were near Hebron (13:18), which is nineteen miles south and somewhat west of Jerusalem. In the time of Herod the Great a wall was built to mark the supposed spot. It is two miles north of Hebron, and the place is called Ramet el-Khalil, with reference to Abraham as the "friend" of God.

Here one day three men approached Abraham's tent. He was sitting at the door of his tent in the heat of the day. When he saw the men he rose and ran to meet them. "My lord," he greeted respectfully the one evidently their leader, and offered them his best hospitality. The description of that hospitality in the Bible record, says one writer, "presents a perfect picture of the manner in which a modern Bedawee sheikh receives travellers arriving at his encampment. He immediately orders his wife or women to make bread, slaughters a sheep or other animal and dresses it in haste; and bringing milk and any other provisions that he may have at hand, with the bread and the meat that he has dressed, sets them before his guests; if they are persons of high rank he also stands by them while they eat."[8]

How high the rank of his visitors was, Abraham only slowly realizes. The Lord has come to declare again his promise. Abraham and Sarah are advanced in age, but in the next spring they will have a son of their own. Also, the Lord is about to disclose his plan to destroy Sodom and Gomorrah.

They go out together, Abraham walking with his visitors to set them on their way. They probably go three miles east of Hebron to the present Beni Na'im, where formerly was a Jewish village called Kephar Barikha, "the village of the blessed one," meaning Abraham. This spot was visited by the pilgrim Paula, who studied with Jerome at Bethlehem at the end of the fourth century A.D. In one of his letters Jerome tells how Paula saw Abraham's oak and went into Hebron. Then: "On the next day soon after sunrise she stood upon the brow of Caphar-barucha..., the point to which Abraham pursued the Lord when he made intercession with Him. And here, as she looked down upon the wide solitude and upon the country once belonging to Sodom and Gomorrah, to Admah and Zeboim, she beheld the balsam vines of Engedi and Zoar. . . . She called to mind the cave in which Lot found refuge, and with tears in her eyes warned the virgins her companions to beware of 'wine wherein is excess.' "⁹

The hills here are over 3000 feet in elevation. Through gaps you can look down upon the Dead Sea, eighteen miles east, 4300 feet below. Here the Lord tells Abraham that he is about to destroy the wicked cities. Here Abraham intercedes for Sodom. He appeals to the righteousness of God to spare the city if fifty righteous are found in it, or forty-five, or forty, or thirty, or twenty, or ten, and the Lord so promises.

The two others, who were angels, went on to Sodom and came there in the evening. Lot was sitting in the gate and rose up first to constrain the visitors to accept the hospitality and, in Sodom, the safety of his home. When all the men of Sodom soon surrounded the house, howling for the visitors to be surrendered to their vice, it was evident that there were none righteous there, not even ten. Placing his duty as a host above his duty as a father, Lot offered his daughters, but the angels averted this calamity when they sealed the house. At dawn they sent Lot, his wife, and two daughters on their way in haste. Not even the two sons-in-law to be, who were to marry the two daughters, would go, for they thought it a jest. But it was no matter for jesting when the cities were utterly destroyed. Even Lot's wife looked back and perished, for there was no time for delay when the hour of doom had come.

That is the story, and now we have to speak of the sites. Where were Sodom and Gomorrah? Ezekiel 16:46 states that Sodom was at the right hand (KJV) of Jerusalem, that is, to the south. More exactly, the location must have been in the Oval of the Jordan, that is, the Lower Jordan valley and the Dead Sea basin, for that is where, according to Genesis 13, Lot looked and chose to go. In Genesis 14 the two cities are linked with three others, and the battle of their five kings with the four invading kings is described as taking place in "the Valley of Siddim (that is, the Salt Sea)." Therefore, some place related to the Salt Sea, which we call the Dead Sea, is indicated, and it is interesting to note that the Arabs have continued to call this body of water the Sea of Lot. Next we are pointed to the south end of the Dead Sea. At the southwest corner there is a range of cliffs five miles long and 600 feet high, made up of layers of marl and salt, eroded into fantastic forms. It was doubtless of this region that Josephus wrote: "I saw the pillar of salt on my travels, for it exists to this day";[10] and it was presumably some unusual salt column in this place which originally gave rise to this feature in the story of Lot. The region of these salt cliffs has long been called Jebel Sudum, or Mount Sodom, so the name has persisted here. But the cities could hardly have been in this area, for there are no suitable locations for towns, and such brooks as come down here are all salty. At the southeast corner of the Dead Sea, however, the situation is different. Here there is a plain along the shore, and here five fresh-water streams come down five separate ravines and make a very fertile region. Perhaps the five towns were on these five streams. Furthermore, the references to Zoar point in this direction. When Lot started out the angels told him to flee to the hills. He protested that that was too far for him to go, and begged to be allowed to go only as far as the town of Zoar, whose name means small. Having left Sodom at dawn, "the sun had risen on the earth when Lot came to Zoar." Zoar is mentioned a number of times in the Old Testament, several times with allusion to a location in the vicinity of Moab, as for example in Isaiah 15:5 where it is said of Moab that "his fugitives flee to Zoar" (compare also Jeremiah 48:4, RSV). Arabic writers also speak of a Zughar, which may have been the same place, as a caravan station on the route between Elath and Jericho. So the hills to which Lot was first told to flee must have been the mountains of Moab, and the small city of Zoar must have been somewhere at the southeast end of the Dead Sea. In his time Josephus says that the place was still called Zoor, and he remarks that it had formed an oasis in the flames for Lot and his daughters.[11]

Consider next the seismic occurrence. What happened to destroy Sodom and Gomorrah? Genesis 19:24-25 describes the destruction in these words: "Then the Lord rained on Sodom and Gomorrah brimstone and fire from the Lord out of heaven; and he overthrew those cities, and all the valley, and all the inhabitants of the cities, and what grew on the ground." Genesis 19:28 also states that Abraham went back to the same place where he had been before and again looked down and now saw that "the smoke of the land went up like the smoke of a furnace." In the description of the destruction, the crucial word appears to be "overthrew," and the same word is also used regularly in other passages which refer to the downfall of the cities. Deuteronomy 29:23, for example, speaks of "an overthrow like that of Sodom and Gomorrah, Admah and Zeboiim, which the Lord overthrew," and from this (compare also Hosea 11:8) we learn incidentally that all four cities, well known to us already from Genesis 14, were involved in the same disaster, although Genesis 18-19, chooses to concentrate on Sodom and Gomorrah. Returning to our recognition of the word "overthrew" as the key term in Genesis 19:25, we might even translate the passage by saying that God "overturned" the cities and the whole plain. This language seems almost certainly to mean that a great earthquake took place. We have already seen that the Jordan River and the Dead Sea are in a deep rift valley. Such a great fault line is of course a likely place for earthquakes. A catalogue of earthquakes in Palestine from 100 B.C. on, has been compiled by D. H. Kallner-Amiran of Hebrew University, Jerusalem, and in the light of his data he says that the whole area of the Jordan rift valley must be considered as of above average earthquake intensity. Furthermore, he shows that one epicenter, or focal point of the earthquakes, is in the general area of the southern part of the Dead Sea and the mountains to the east of it, because at this point the rift valley intersects with the main axis of the Beer-sheba basin which is the main structural border in the geology of Palestine west of the Jordan.[12] The area just indicated is precisely that in which we have located in probability the cities which were destroyed. While the investigation just cited does not reach back to the ancient time with which we are concerned, the data of later times make all the more likely the supposition of an earthquake centered at the southern part of the Dead Sea as the cause of the "overthrow" of Sodom and Gomorrah. To correspond with the indications of the biblical account, such a seismic occurrence must have been of far greater than usual intensity. With such a supposition in mind, it is a natural question to inquire whether there is evidence anywhere else in the Near East for a major catastrophe of this nature in the time with which we are presumably here concerned. Significantly enough, there is in fact archeological evidence for a colossal earthquake which destroyed the palaces of Crete and the cities of Ugarit and Alalakh (Level VII) in Syria at a time around 1650 B.C.[13] Since the battle of the kings in the valley of Siddim (which is the Salt Sea) came probably somewhat after 1700 B.C., as we saw previously, and since the destruction of the cities was an event which followed yet some time after that, the date of approximately 1650 B.C. would be satisfactory for the fall of Sodom and Gomorrah. In that case it was indeed a vastly destructive seismic occurrence which overthrew the biblical cities and reached to the northeastern Mediterranean as well.

What about the brimstone and fire, and the smoke that went up like the smoke of a furnace? Fire is a natural and usual concomitant of earthquake. With a major shift in the earth's surface, natural gases might have been released and ignited. Brimstone is sulphur, and there are deposits of sulphur and bitumen all around the south end of the Dead Sea. Josephus even tells of how black masses of bitumen floated on the surface of Lake Asphaltitis, as he calls the Dead Sea.[14] The natural conditions were evidently at hand for a tremendous conflagration.

Yet again we must ask about the submersion of the cities. Where are the infamous cities now? The note in Genesis 14:3 which states that the valley of Siddim where the kings fought is the Salt Sea, suggests that the plain itself was submerged beneath the Dead Sea. The statement is equivalent, in fact, to saying that what was then the valley of Siddim is now the Dead Sea. Geologically, the strata of the west shore of the Dead Sea are displaced by more than three hundred feet in height in comparison with the east side. Although we do not know when that happened, it seems very well possible that the plain which now lies something like twelve feet beneath the surface of the shallow southern part of the Dead Sea could have sunk and been submerged due to earthquake.[15] In that case, the ruins of Sodom and Gomorrah, Admah and Zeboiim, lie even now beneath those waters.

In 1960 Dr. Ralph E. Baney, Baptist missionary from Kansas City, Missouri, was reported to have used skin-diving methods in the Dead Sea in an effort to locate the ruins of the cities, but whether any dependable results were obtained is, at this writing, still uncertain. Underwater exploration is a feature of modern work by recognized archeologists, as for example at Caesarea on the Palestine coast, but in the case of the Dead Sea attempt Nelson Glueck is quoted as expressing the opinion that the thick salt deposits on the bottom would make it impossible to get to the remains.[16] That the ruins of the cities remain, at least presently, inaccessible to us only emphasizes the completeness of the destruction which was visited upon them.

Having asked and answered as best we know to do the question as to what happened to Sodom and Gomorrah, we may also wonder if anything similar can happen now? Man can, at any rate, still be very wicked. The unnatural vice of the Sodomites was not obliterated by the destruction of their city, but is found later in Judges 19 and I Kings 14, and it is still protested against in the pagan world of his time by Paul in Romans 1. Indeed in the form sodomy, the name of the city is still attached to the unnatural vice with which the law must deal and with which papers and books are perhaps too often occupied. In this and other ways men can still be very wicked.

Civilization can also be destroyed. Our final view of Lot is obtained in Genesis 19. He has now gone up out of Zoar, the little oasis from the flames, to dwell in the hills with his two

daughters. And, as Genesis 19:30 tells us, they dwelt in a cave.
The man who chose the city has returned to the cave. Will this
be a parable of modern man? Having moved into the great
cities, will he see them destroyed as the wickedness of his own
deeds comes up against the righteous laws of the righteous God?
Will he himself be reduced again to a cave existence? In a
recent novel called *The Descent* Gina Berriault describes the
situation she imagines in the year 1964: Peace talks are continuing in Washington and in the United Nations. The United
States of America has even established a new post in the cabinet
—a Secretary for Humanity. But the pace and proportion of the
bomb and missile race is such that the terrified population is
now engaged in a mass building program of underground shel-
ters. To these, frightened people will scurry when the bombs
begin to fall. Will this be the fate of modern man?

Yet in view of the story of Lot and of Sodom and Gomorrah,
we must not fail to ask, too, if God, then and now, delivers the
righteous? By our standards, Lot was a man of mixed character.
The church fathers often debated the merit of what he did. Did
he do wrongly when he put his duty as a host above his duty as
a father? Most of us would say he did. Certainly he brought
most of his troubles upon himself. Yet in comparison with his
day and over against the inhabitants of Sodom, he does stand
out. He was hospitable, as his uncle before him was. Hebrews
13:2 was probably thinking of both Abraham and Lot in the
exhortation: "Do not neglect to show hospitality to strangers
for thereby some have entertained angels unawares." II Peter 2:7
even calls him "righteous," and says that he was "greatly distressed by the licentiousness of the wicked" and that he was
"vexed in his righteous soul day after day with their lawless
deeds." And Lot did do what the divine command told him to
do. So a man marked by ambiguities of character indeed, but
also by at least a measure of trust in God, was the recipient of

the mercy of God. The ultimate reason of his deliverance is stated in Genesis 19:16: "The Lord being merciful unto him." God did rescue him. For the comfort and encouragement of the persecuted Christians of his day, and of all who put their trust in God in all times, II Peter draws the conclusion: "And if he rescued righteous Lot . . . then the Lord knows how to rescue the godly from trial."

10 THE SACRIFICE (ALMOST) OF ISAAC (Genesis 20-23)

As we continue to trace the biblical narrative of the patriarchs, we find that Abraham and Sarah, his wife, finally had a son of their own. Abraham had come to Canaan in faith in God's promise that he would have both land and descendants. Aside, however, from Ishmael, borne by Hagar, the Egyptian slave girl, he had hitherto had no offspring. When God reiterated the promise, Abraham and Sarah could not help laughing, it seemed so unlikely at their advanced age. When a son was actually born, with Abraham one hundred years of age and Sarah ninety-one, Sarah said that God had in fact "made laughter" (Genesis 21:6) for her in her old age. So they called the child "laughter," for that is what the name Isaac means in the Hebrew language. But when Isaac was a lad, the shadow of a terrible happening almost extinguished the laughter. The story of this event is told in Genesis 22. It is one of the most moving and touching stories in the Bible. S. R. Driver says of it: "The narrative is told simply, but with singular pathos and dignity";[1] and John Skinner calls it "a literary masterpiece," and says that it "is told with exquisite simplicity; every sentence vibrates with restrained emotion, which shows how fully the

112

author realizes the tragic horror of the situation."[2]

We will consider first what the story tells us about the world of that time. Abraham almost sacrificed Isaac. It was a world in which human sacrifice was practiced. Such a practice has in fact been known in many places. The *Encyclopaedia of Religion and Ethics* edited by James Hastings devotes fifty-five columns to the subject. We need look only at the more immediate environment of Abraham. In studying the life of Abraham we have already noted that he came from Ur, in Lower Mesopotamia, and that at that place a large cemetery has been found, dating probably around 2500 B.C. and containing a wealth of gold vessels and precious jewelry. Because of this wealth, the excavator, C. Leonard Woolley, surmised that the chief personages buried here were kings and queens; others suppose them to have been priests and priestesses. For our present purpose, the important point is to note that along with the chief persons, many others were buried too, so many that the tombs have been called "death pits." In the tomb of Lady Shub-ad were the remains of twenty-five other people; in that of A-bar-gi were the remains of more than sixty; and in yet another tomb were the remains of six men and sixty-eight women. These have the appearance of attendants who went to death as human sacrifices along with their lords and ladies. When Abraham came down from Northwest Mesopotamia to Canaan, he passed the area where the Phoenicians were to live later. Eusebius says that the Phoenicians offered human sacrifice, and in the excavations at Byblus there is to be seen, in the obelisk temple, an altar believed to have been used for that purpose. Abraham also visited Egypt. In Egypt a well-known monument is the temple of Philae, now mostly inundated by the Nile. Procopius states that in that temple human victims were offered to the sun. Thus in the lands which surrounded Abraham and in the times from long before to long after his day, human sacrifice was a practice.

There was not only human sacrifice in general but also child sacrifice in particular, and that even in Canaan. Judges 11:30 states that the early Israelite judge Jephthah offered his daughter to pay a vow he made before he went to war. II Kings 16:3 records that a king of Judah, Ahaz, "even burned his son as an offering." II Kings 17:17 says of the apostate people of Israel that "they burned their sons and their daughters as offerings." II Kings 21:6 states that Manasseh, king in Jerusalem, "burned his son as an offering." It seems likely that such actions were usually in imitation of "the abominations of the heathen," as is explicitly said in regard to Manasseh; it is also evident that such influences were a real factor in Canaan.

Child sacrifice included specifically the sacrifice of the first-born, and this can be seen without and within Canaan. When the battle was going against him, Mesha king of Moab "took his eldest son who was to reign in his stead and offered him for a burnt offering upon the wall" (II Kings 3:27). When Hiel of Bethel rebuilt Jericho, "he laid its foundation at the cost of Abiram his first-born" (I Kings 16:34). Perhaps the skeleton of a girl of about fifteen found built into the wall, in the excavation of Megiddo, represents such a foundation sacrifice.

Look at the immediate environment of Abraham. At this time he was at Beer-sheba (Genesis 21:33; 22:19). Beer-sheba was on the edge of the Negeb. In his history of this region, called *Rivers in the Desert,* Nelson Glueck states that child sacrifice had been practiced there since the Chalcolithic period and still was practiced in the Middle Bronze Age which, we have seen, was the time of Abraham. At Tell Abu Matar, near Beer-sheba, the skeleton of a newborn babe was under a fireplace, and the skeleton of a child lay under a stone wall, presumably as a foundation offering. Glueck writes of this melancholy custom, and then points to Abraham, in these words:

The firstborn of man and woman were offered to the gods so that the hearth might be full, the women conceive easily and bear many sons, the tilled acres yield their crops in unfailing abundance, the herds and flocks increase with numberless calves and lambs and kids, the newly built house be full of blessing. Such gifts were intended to placate their wrath or elicit their favor. Generation after generation throughout centuries and millennia repeated this pitiful rite. Then somehow in the midst of the remote fastness of Sinai, a still small voice penetrated the innermost consciousness of man.[3]

Let us consider, then, what the story tells us about the faith of Abraham. He almost sacrificed Isaac because he believed it was what God wanted him to do. This shows that he was willing to go to the limit for what he believed was right. Isaac was precious to him. This was true personally. Isaac was the first and only son of Abraham and Sarah. He was the son they had believed they would never be able to have. He was the son who had brought them joy, whose name was "laughter." In Genesis 22:2 he is explicitly called Abraham's "only son." Isaac was precious too in relation to the promise. God had promised Abraham descendants. The only hope for that promise was through this son. If Abraham was willing to give up this son, he was willing to give up the dearest he had.

This obedience to what he understood as the will of God is what later writers saw in Abraham that was so great. Hebrews 11:17-18 pointed out that he had a loyalty for which he was willing to give everything: "By faith Abraham, when he was tested, offered up Isaac, and he who had received the promises was ready to offer up his only son, of whom it was said, Through Isaac shall your descendants be named." James 2:21 observed that Abraham did the deed which demonstrated his faith: "Was not Abraham our father justified by works, when he offered his son Isaac upon the altar?" Philo emphasized in contrast with the

heathen sacrifices of his contemporaries the moral superiority of
the sacrifice of Abraham:

It was not offered from any selfish motive, under the compul-
sion of a tyrant, or through fear of man, from desire of present
glory or hope of future renown. He did not offer his son to win
a battle, or to avert a famine or a pestilence, or to obtain some
coveted gift of the gods. Nor did he give up one child out of
many. He was ready to sacrifice his only son, his beloved son,
the son of his old age, and he did this simply because God commanded it. His sacrifice in itself went far beyond all heathen
sacrifices, as in its motives it infinitely surpassed them. He gave
all that he had, and he gave it not from fear, or from interest,
but out of love to God.[4]

But we must consider too what the story tells us about the
will of God. The account begins (Genesis 22:1) with the statement that God tempted or tested Abraham. The crucial Hebrew
word in this statement may be translated "tempt," as it is in the
King James Version. In the Septuagint it is rendered by the same
Greek word as is found in James 1:13 which states that "God . . .
tempts no one." Following this line of thought, we may say
that the writer of the account in Genesis was wrong in stating
that God tempted Abraham, that James gives us the true insight, namely, that God himself tempts no one, and that therefore what actually happened was that Abraham was tempted by
his environment. How that could have been we have already
given sufficient evidence to show. Abraham saw others going to
this terrible extreme of the sacrifice of the first-born. He believed
that he should do likewise. He was willing to do as much for his
God as any man would do for the deity he believed in. So
while it was not true that God actually wanted him to do this,
it was undoubtedly true that, at this stage, Abraham fully believed that God wanted him to do it.

The Hebrew word in question may also be translated "test."
This is how it is rendered in the Revised Standard Version of

Genesis 22:1, and also how the corresponding Greek word is translated in Hebrews 11:17 (even the King James Version, which uses "tempt" in James 1:13, employs "try" in Hebrews 11:17). Following the line of thought suggested by the word "test," we may say that God, who is ultimately responsible for all things, allowed that environment to exist and allowed Abraham to be in it; therefore, he did in fact allow such a test of Abraham to take place.

The main point of what the story has to tell as to the will of God must, however, surely be sought in the conclusion and climax of the account. Abraham saddled his donkey, and took with him two of his young men, his son Isaac, and wood cut for a burnt offering. They journeyed unto the third day, to a place in the land of Moriah. If the place here indicated is the same as the Mount Moriah mentioned in II Chronicles 3:1, it was where Solomon's temple was later built. In 1838 it took Robinson over twenty hours to go by camel from Beer-sheba to Jerusalem, so three days for Abraham's journey on foot is a reasonable length of time. Nelson Glueck, on the other hand, thinks there would have been no need to carry firewood to this place, and supposes rather that the land of Moriah was somewhere in the severe and unforested ranges of Sinai. Finally, the two young men and the donkey were left behind, and Abraham and Isaac went on together. Isaac now carried the wood, while Abraham had fire and knife. "My father," asked Isaac as they went along, "where is the lamb for a burnt offering?" Abraham, his heart breaking, replied, "God will provide." At the place Abraham built an altar, one supposes of stones. He laid the wood on it, then bound Isaac and laid him thereupon. The knife was raised and the fire ready. At that moment the angel of the Lord called the name of Abraham twice, and when Abraham hearkened, commanded him not to lay his hand on the lad. Abraham looked around him, and saw a ram caught in a thicket by his horns.

He took the ram and offered it as a burnt offering instead of his son. Then he called the name of that place "The Lord will provide."

Of the significance of this climax of the account, F. W. Robertson wrote:

We must take the history as a whole, the conclusion as well as the commencement. The sacrifice of Isaac was commanded at first, and forbidden at the end. Had it ended in Abraham's accomplishing the sacrifice, I know not what could have been said; it would have left on the page of Scripture a dark and painful blot. My reply to God's *seeming* to require human sacrifice is the conclusion of this chapter. God says, "Lay not thine hand upon the lad." This is the final decree. Thus human sacrifices were *distinctly* forbidden. He *really* required the surrender of the father's will. He *seemed* to demand the sacrifice of life.[5]

What Abraham learned in this tremendously vivid object lesson, as it might be called, and what is taught in this so moving story, was never forgotten by the people of Israel. It is true that upon occasion and under pagan influence, as we have seen above, kings and people sometimes fell back into the abominable practice of human sacrifice, but this was nevermore an accepted part of the life of Israel. Leviticus 18:21 legislates against the practice: "You shall not give any of your children to devote them by fire to Molech, and so profane the name of your God." When it occurred, the prophets were swift to condemn as Jeremiah did when he wrote: "They have filled this place with the blood of innocents, and have built the high places of Baal to burn their sons in the fire" (19:5); and as Ezekiel did when he said: "When you . . . sacrifice your sons by fire, you defile yourselves with all your idols" (20:31). The only acceptable sacrifice in Israel was the animal sacrifice, and when at last the temple was destroyed, this too ceased. There remains only the usage, at the Jewish New Year Festival, of the blowing

of the shophar, or ram's horn, and this act has its origin in the
Isaac story.

It is proper also to consider what the story tells about the nature of Isaac. One Jewish rabbi thought the event under consideration took place immediately after Isaac was weaned; others
calculated from the Scriptures that Sarah died when Isaac was
thirty-seven years old and, supposing that her death was caused
by the shock of this very happening, concluded that Isaac was
of this age at the time. The Bible, however, calls Isaac a "lad"
and, since he was large enough to carry the load of wood, yet
obviously younger than the two "young men" who were taken
along, we may picture him as of just such age as we too would
mean by saying "lad." Concerning the lad, it seems evident that
the narrative intends to emphasize his submission and obedience
as well as the faith of Abraham. Isaac is tractable and trusting.
He trudges up to the place with the heavy load of wood upon
his back. He wonders what will happen, but accepts his father's
word. Evidently without a struggle, he allows himself to be
bound and laid on the altar. The particular Hebrew word translated "bound" which is used here does not appear elsewhere in
the Old Testament, but in post-biblical Hebrew it is the same
word which means specifically to bind the bent legs of an animal for sacrifice.

The trustful and obedient nature of Isaac is brought out in one
of the early plays which have come down to us from before the
time of Shakespeare. Known as *The Brome Abraham and Isaac,*
this must have been played at about the time Columbus discovered America, for there is a copy of it in a book which bears
the date 1499. In a scene filled with pathos, Abraham and
Isaac converse in this manner:

Abraham.
I am full sorry, son, thy blood to spill,
But truly, my child, it is not as I please.

Isaac.

Now I would to God my mother were here on this hill!
She would kneel for me on both her knees
To save my life.
And since that my mother is not here,
Change your look, I pray you, father dear,
And kill me not with your knife.

Abraham.

Forsooth, my son, save I thee kill,
I should grieve God right sore, I fear,
It is his commandment and also his will
That I should do this same deed here.

He commanded me, son, for certain
To make my sacrifice with thy blood.

Isaac.

And is it God's will that I should be slain?

Abraham.

Yea, truly, Isaac, my son so good,
And therefore my hands I wring!

Isaac.

Now, father, against my Lord's decree,
I will never murmur, loud or still.
He might have sent me a better destiny,
If it had been his will.

Abraham.

Forsooth, son, save this deed I did,
In grievous displeasure our Lord would be.

Isaac.

Nay, nay, father, God forbid
That ever ye should grieve him for me!
. . . .
I pray you, father, no more your grief renew,
For, if I am once dead and gone from you,

I shall soon be out of your mind.
Therefore do our Lord's bidding,
And when I am dead, then pray for me.
But, good father, tell ye my mother nothing,
Say that I am in another country dwelling.[6]

It is small wonder that the early church writers saw in Isaac a type of Christ. Jesus, too, trudged up the mount, carrying the wood upon his back, and was bound on it, uncomplaining. The Son accepted the Father's will; the Father gave the Son. Paul may have been thinking of Abraham and Isaac when he wrote in Romans 8:32 about God's giving of Jesus that he "did not spare his own Son but gave him up for us all." The Epistle of Barnabas (Chapter 7) speaks of "the type established in Isaac when he was offered upon the altar," and Irenaeus and Augustine make similar references.

Yet Isaac was not only a type of the sacrifice of Christ, he was also a symbol of deliverance. In this sense the picture of Isaac is one of the oldest and most frequent paintings in the Christian catacombs beneath Rome. As do the other subjects so often painted there, this representation says that even in the greatest extremity, God is able to deliver. Thus a brave and trusting lad of long ago became a source of hope and confidence to many.

Finally, consider what the story says to us and about us. It says that we must be ready to make any required sacrifice to God. But it also says that we must use every means to know for sure what it is that God wishes us to do. It is possible to do terrible things, believing that it is the will of God. If we need to do God's will, we need also to know as well as we can what that will really is. Walter Russell Bowie says: "The ways of God are sometimes hidden and at first not understood; but ultimately his will is found to be not contradictory to the purest emotions planted in human souls."[7] When that is understood, a father and his little lad can go home together, together trusting and obeying a good God.

11 CLIMBING JACOB'S LADDER WITH HIM (Genesis 24-36)

In what has gone before, we have dealt with Abraham and Isaac, and now we come to Jacob, the third of the patriarchs. From the eleventh chapter of Genesis it will be remembered that Abraham had two brothers Haran and Nahor. Haran died early and left the son Lot, whom Abraham took with him to Canaan, and also two daughters Milcah and Iscah. Nahor is not mentioned as going with Abraham, but evidently went later as far as Northwest Mesopotamia, where we read of the city of Nahor not only in the Old Testament but also, under the name Nakhur, in the cuneiform texts from Mari. When Abraham, at a subsequent time, wanted to obtain a wife for his son Isaac, he sent his servant to the city of Nahor. Nahor had married Milcah and their son, the nephew of Abraham, was Bethuel. His children, in turn, were Laban and Rebekah, and it was Rebekah who was brought back to be the wife of Isaac. Isaac and Rebekah had twins, Esau and Jacob, and it is with them that we are presently concerned, particularly with Jacob, and particularly with the most famous event in his life when he saw the ladder.

The ladder which Jacob saw represents, for one thing, the ladder of the discovery of the presence of God in an unexpected place. The event of the ladder came about in the following way. Sometimes twins are so much alike that one can hardly tell them apart; sometimes they are so different one can hardly believe they are twins. In this case Esau and Jacob were very different. They were different in appearance. Esau was ruddy and hairy; Jacob was smooth and civilized. They were different in interest. Esau was an active man of the outdoors, a man of the field and a skillful hunter; Jacob was a quiet man who liked the comfort of his tent, and even liked to cook. They were also different in their status. Esau was the favorite of his father; Jacob was the favorite of his mother.

The two sons were not only different, they also became rivals. They became rivals for something which Esau had but did not care much about, and which Jacob did not have but did care about. This was the official right of being the oldest son. Strictly speaking Esau was, by a few seconds, the older of the two, for he was the first to come into the world. But he did not think much about what this meant. Jacob was not the older, but he wished he were, and he evidently thought much about what it meant. God had made a promise to Abraham. He had renewed that promise to Isaac. He would undoubtedly renew it yet again to Isaac's oldest son. To be the son who would head the family as time went on, to be the one through whom God's promise would work, meant much to this quiet man who took time to think about these things.

So Jacob attempted to secure that right, and he succeeded. It was related that he made the attempt even at the time of birth. Although he was the second of the twins to come into the world, Jacob already had his hand on Esau's heel as if he were trying to pull him back and take his place. Later when he was grown up, Jacob was cooking pottage and Esau came in from the field, famished. The pottage was made of lentils, a small leguminous plant cultivated in all parts of ancient Palestine for food.

To judge from later custom, at least, the lentils were often stewed along with onions, rice, oil, or small bits of meat and fat, and well seasoned. As the pleasing aroma of this tasty dish attracted the notice of hungry Esau, Jacob shrewdly suggested an exchange of pottage for birthright. To Esau it was a good enough bargain. He ate and drank with gusto, and went his way. Thus he "despised his birthright" (Genesis 25:34). Again later when Isaac was so old he could not even see, he intended to give his official blesssing to his oldest (and favorite) son. This time Jacob (put up to it by his mother) successfully impersonated his brother and received the blesssing. But now Esau, who had evidently had time to reflect upon his earlier foolishness, was greatly distressed. His father, however, could not take back his words. Esau decided, therefore, that as soon as the father died he would kill Jacob.

That was when Jacob left home. Again it was Rebekah who thought up the plan, and it was a plausible and valid one. Like his father, Jacob too should have a wife from among their own people in Northwest Mesopotamia. This was doubly desirable, for Esau had married two Hittite women there in Canaan and they had made life bitter for their parents-in-law. Jacob should go himself to find and obtain this wife. So Jacob starts out as a lonely traveler on a mission of uncertain outcome. The young man who has depended too much on his mother's care goes forth from beneath her protecting care. Although she tells him that it will be but a few days and that when his brother's wrath subsides she will send for him to come back, he knows that it will not be so short a time as that. In fact the time was twenty years, and his mother was evidently dead and buried before he came back. The civilized man who liked the comfort of a tent must now seek his rest where he can find it, lying down at night in the stony fields he traverses. The domestic man who cooked the savory pottage must now depend upon what he can obtain en route. The quiet man must now go out into the rough world.

The way was long. On the map the distance is 400 miles; the terrain was rugged and the climate fairly severe. Jacob started from Beer-sheba in the extreme south of Palestine, went north probably past Hebron and Jerusalem and came to the vicinity of Luz. This place, twelve miles north of Jerusalem, and later known as Bethel, was already occupied as a town, according to recent excavations, in the twenty-first century B.C., several centuries before the time of Jacob. Once Abraham had pitched his tent and built an altar in the vicinity. Today an Arab village still marks the place, and even the ancient name has been preserved in the somewhat modified form of Beitin instead of Bethel.

Here, several nights out from home, and not in the town but out in a field, the lone wanderer made his bivouac. He took one of the stones of the place (and in almost any place in Palestine there are plenty of stones), put it under his head, and lay down to sleep. Save that Abraham had once worshiped God here, which Jacob may not even have known, this barren spot was an unlikely enough place for anything special to happen. Save that he had wanted to be his father's heir in respect to the covenant, Jacob was an unlikely enough person to whom anything special might happen. After all, he had deceived his father and defrauded his brother. And, by his own later testimony, he was not expecting anything special to happen. But something did happen, something unexpected and wonderful. Jacob dreamed. In the dream he saw a ladder set up on earth and the top reached the heaven. The angels of God were ascending and descending on it. The Lord stood above it, and said, "I am the God of Abraham and Isaac," and he renewed the covenant promise to Jacob that the land should belong to him and his descendants. He also said: "I am with you and will keep you wherever you go, and will bring you back to this land" (Genesis 28:15). When Jacob awoke, he said: "Surely the Lord is in this place; and I did not

know it." The place was suddenly awesome. It was "none other
than the house of God, and . . . the gate of heaven." So he set
up the very stone he had been sleeping on, for a memorial, and
consecrated it by pouring some oil on it. He called the place
Bethel, which means "the house of God."

Since this is what happened to Jacob, we too, if we are going
to climb Jacob's ladder with him, must discover God's presence
even in unexpected places. We are often enough like Jacob in
our essential position, lonely travelers in what seems an empty
land, on an uncertain mission. Changing the figure slightly,
George Arthur Buttrick has spoken of life as "the lonely voyage."[1]
In this connection he recalls a memoir of Rupert Brooke. Brooke
was taking a ship from Liverpool to New York. Suddenly he felt
lonely. Apparently he was the only passenger with no one to
wave good-by to him. He ran down the gangplank and found a
boy. Inquiring his name, he gave him sixpence, told him he was
to be his friend, and asked him to wave to him when the ship
departed. But if many people have been in Jacob's lonely position, many too have in some manner experienced with him the
discovery of God's unexpected presence. So it was with Francis
Thompson, sad and lonely in London, but writing of Jacob's
ladder "pitched betwixt Heaven and Charing Cross." So it was
with the people of the Negro spirituals who sang "We are climbing Jacob's ladder." So it was with the man whose strange
story Dr. Buttrick also tells in concluding his discussion of "the
lonely voyage." Almost every night this man dreamed of falling
into a bottomless void. In one of its stanzas, his school hymn
had made him sing of living so that he would dread the grave
as little as his bed, but now there was nothing he dreaded more
than to retire and face the prospect of that recurrent dream. One
day in a cemetery, however, he saw an inscription on a grave
which cited Deuteronomy 33:27 in the affirmation that the
eternal God is our home, and underneath are the everlasting

arms. Then and there the wonder took place. Faith came to him, and the nightly horror of the dreadful dream was banished.

The Hebrew word translated "ladder" in Genesis 28:12 does not occur elsewhere in the Bible, and some have suggested that it might have the meaning of "stair." At all events it seems to mean something which provides a series of steps and a way of ascent. The Bible does not use this word in telling about any more of the experiences of Jacob, but one wonders if the remembrance of that ladder seen at Bethel did not stay with him and help him in following days when he faced not a few steep and hard ascents. There was, for example, the ladder of long work for a deeply desired goal. Jacob came on the hundreds of miles to Paddan-aram, to Haran, and to the home of Laban, his mother's brother. He met and loved Rachel, daughter of Laban. He entered into a hard agreement to work for Laban seven years for Rachel. "So Jacob served seven years for Rachel, and they seemed to him but a few days because of the love he had for her" (Genesis 29:20). Then crafty Laban, trying to make sure his older and evidently less attractive daughter Leah did not remain at home unmarried, passed her off on Jacob first, and for Rachel he required seven more years of work. That was fourteen years of labor, but a true love made them swift and light. Even so, if we are going to climb Jacob's ladder with him we may have to work a long time for something we deeply desire and consider worth having. Helen Traubel, back of whose success as a noted singer must lie long, hard, and patient effort for the mastery of her art, says that the fundamental secret of her life lies in the three words taught her by her mother when she was a small child, namely, "Make haste slowly." Such is the nature of the steep ascent in the lives of many people who share with Jacob something of his demanding experience. Such, too, is what the Negro spiritual knows when it speaks of how "every round goes higher, higher."

There was also the ladder of struggle with unscrupulous opposition. We have already seen one example of how Laban treated Jacob when he gave him Leah instead of Rachel. After Jacob finished his fourteen years he wanted to depart. But Laban knew he had been a very valuable worker, and wanted to keep him. So he made a new agreement. Jacob was to be paid with a particular portion of the increase of the flock, the portion which by every normal expectation, and by Laban's planned manipulations too, would be small. Here, however, it came out that the increase actually favored Jacob. After six more years, twenty in all, Jacob again desired to go. Now as he reviewed the past in which he had worked fourteen years for the two daughters whom he received in marriage, and six years for the flock, he could count ten times when Laban had changed his wages. Finally, lest even then Laban send him away empty-handed, he had to flee with family and goods while Laban was absent at sheep shearing. In his earlier life Jacob had been involved in deceit, but in all of these later events he seems to have been substantially honest and a man of integrity. Even the fact that Rachel carried off the household gods and hid them when her father came after them and tried to get them back, appears in a somewhat different light from the Nuzi texts where we learn that possession of the household gods meant right to the property and Rachel and Leah said that their father had long since come to regard themselves as foreigners, was using up the money given for them, and no longer preserved any portion or inheritance for them. Therefore, they had to do what they could to safeguard their rights. So Jacob, who did not even know about the household gods, could at last confront Laban with honest indignation. He, Jacob, had kept his part of the agreement. He had given faithful service. Laban had prospered because of him. And Laban had to acknowledge that it was so. If we are climbing Jacob's ladder with him, therefore, we have to try to meet unscrupulous opposition with honesty and integrity.

There was the ladder too of wrestling with a higher power. Although twenty years had gone by, there was still an anxiety in the mind of Jacob and a burden on his conscience. He had wronged Esau, now he was going home and would meet him. In his anxiety he made various arrangements: to divide his company so that if some were destroyed some might escape; to send presents ahead to placate the presumably angry brother; to keep his dearest family members in the safest position. In his burdened conscience he was left alone at the ford of the river Jabbok to wrestle with an unknown assailant. If we ask who that unknown antagonist was, we can hardly think of this as anything less than the manifestation of the God of righteousness himself. Walter Russell Bowie writes about Jacob at this juncture: "Before he could ever be at peace with himself and with his world, he would have to come to grips with the facts of his past experience—and with the invisible power of the righteousness he had violated—and wrestle with them for his life."[2] This Jacob did here, and here he received a new name—Israel, which means "he who strives with God." So, if we are going along Jacob's way with him, we may someday have to wrestle with the God of righteousness.

The ladder of the working out of reconciliation also comes into our view. As we have seen, Jacob approached his meeting with Esau with great apprehension. When he heard that Esau was coming with four hundred men he was terrified. He bowed himself seven times to the ground as he moved toward the encounter. Jacob has at last humbled himself. But Esau ran to meet him, embraced him, kissed him, and they wept together. Esau was, after all, a warmhearted, spontaneous man. What Jacob took from him was a responsibility if an honor. It was something he had never really cared very much about anyway. He was as casual and easygoing as ever. Perhaps he had not forgotten, but he had long since stopped bothering himself about what Jacob had done. So at last Jacob came up what was perhaps the hardest ladder of all to climb, the one he had to humble himself to ascend, the ladder of reconciliation. That the reconciliation was permanent we are glad to deduce from the fact that when their father Isaac, then one hundred and eighty years old, breathed his last, Esau and Jacob together buried him. If we are climbing Jacob's ladder with him, we may need to humble ourselves in some reconciliation.

There was finally the ladder of worship. Jacob came thus again to Canaan. At Shechem he purchased land and pitched his tent. There he erected an altar and called it El-Elohe-Israel, God, the God of Israel. Thus he remembered and honored the God who had kept his promise and brought him safely home again. And if we climb life's way with Jacob, we will mark the way with altars of remembrance and thankfulness, altars to God, the God of Israel.

12 THE PROVIDENCE OF GOD IN JOSEPH'S LIFE AND OURS
(Genesis 37-50)

In the story of Joseph, which occupies Chapters 37-50 of the book of Genesis, we have a dramatic biography. To have such, we must have a stirring life and an effective narrative concerning it. Here we certainly have both. This person had remarkable experiences. The story concerning him is longer and more detailed than any previously encountered in Genesis. It must have been told many times, perhaps in two slightly different forms, probably orally at first and afterward written down. The delineation of character and the tracing of the forces at work make the account of gripping interest. It challenges us to try to understand, for our own lives, the meaning of what happened in the life of this man.

We remember that the immediate forebears of Joseph were Abraham his great grandfather, Isaac his grandfather, and Jacob his father. Jacob had twelve sons and, since Jacob's other name was Israel, these twelve were the children of Israel and as such they were also the ancestors of the collective and continuing children of Israel or Israelite people. A concise family list is given in Genesis 35:22-26: "Now the sons of Jacob were twelve. The sons of Leah: Reuben (Jacob's first-born), Simeon, Levi, Judah,

131

Issachar, and Zebulun. The sons of Rachel: Joseph and Benjamin. The sons of Bilhah, Rachel's maid: Dan and Naphtali. The sons of Zilpah, Leah's maid: Gad and Asher. These were the sons of Jacob who were born to him in Paddan-aram."

In what we might call Act I of the drama of Joseph's life, disaster strikes a precocious youth. Joseph was the favorite son of his father. Among the four women who were the mothers of his children, Rachel was Jacob's really beloved wife. For her he worked for fourteen years and, even after that, it was evidently not soon that Joseph was born, for he is described as the son of his father's old age. It is true that in the family record given above, Rachel is listed with two sons, Joseph and Benjamin, and it is said of the entire group of twelve that they were born in Paddan-aram where Jacob worked so long. Actually it is tacitly understood, as told shortly before, that the second son of Rachel, Benjamin, was only born later still when the family was in Canaan and moving toward Bethlehem. It seems probable, therefore, that for a considerable length of time (and some think possibly even until the time when he was sold), Joseph was the only son of Jacob by his really beloved wife. Furthermore, when the second son of Rachel, Benjamin, was born, the mother died. If this happened while Joseph was still at home, it could only accentuate the attachment of the father to Joseph, for this son and the newborn baby, in whose arrival the mother's life had been lost, were all he now had left of Rachel. If, as we may easily imagine, Joseph had the features of his mother, the attachment of the lonely heart of Jacob to this son is the more readily understood. Jacob's own mother Rebekah had been partial to him and had done favoritistic things, such as putting him up to stealing the blessing of Isaac their father from Esau his brother. Now Jacob in turn did not hide his favoritism. The most open, but doubtless not the only, mark of it was the "coat of many colors" (Genesis 37:3, KJV) which he made for him. According to some manuscripts this was "a long robe with sleeves" (RSV), and according to II Samuel 13:18 such garments were worn by members of kings' families. Egyptian paintings from about this very time (in a Theban tomb of the fifteenth century B.C.) show high-ranking Canaanites wearing robes made of cloth pieces stitched together with colorful embroidery, red, blue, and brown; sometimes the cloth was of different color inside and out and, worn in folds, gave a multicolored appearance. Something of this sort may have been the fine garment in which Joseph was attired.

Joseph was also the favored son among the brothers. We have advanced the suggestion that Joseph may have resembled his mother, and she was "beautiful and lovely" (Genesis 29:17); so Joseph probably was well favored in physical stature and appearance, and this is confirmed when later he is described as "handsome and good-looking" (Genesis 39:6). Some of the brothers were probably showing the evidences of age by now; Joseph, however, was at what might be the very best period of his youth, seventeen years of age (Genesis 37:2). Above all, Joseph was now being singled out by dreams in which his superiority to his brothers and their subservience to him, either present or future, were indicated.

This favorite, favored son was also the forward son. The word "precocious" refers to early developed talents and in that sense seems applicable to Joseph. The same word can also mean "too forward" in some respect, and one is afraid that it is applicable to Joseph in that meaning too. He not only had the dreams which we just mentioned, he also told them outright to his brothers. They hated him already because of his father's favoritism (Genesis 37:4); now they hated him more than ever because of the dreams (Genesis 37:5).

The foregoing is what set the stage for the disaster. The disaster struck in the following way. The brothers were out pasturing their father's flock. From early until recent times the shepherds

of Palestine have been accustomed to go through the land from
south to north, seeking the best grazing for their animals. So the
brothers went from Hebron to Shechem and on north to Dothan,
at the north end of the mountains. This area is described as a
"wilderness," but the Hebrew word *midbar* means a "driving-
place" for flocks, hence can indicate good pasture ground. Here,
too, probably cisterns provided for storage of water. Dothan itself is a *tell*, excavated now since 1953 and shown to have been
continuously occupied from the beginning of the Canaanite
period to the end of the Israelite age, 3000 to 600 B.C., hence it
was a town at the time of Joseph. Now Joseph was sent on an
errand from Jacob his father to find where the brothers were and
how they were doing. When they saw him coming they conspired
to slay him, but Reuben, the eldest, persuaded the others just
to cast him into a pit, presumably one of the cisterns that was
empty. Reuben intended to come back and get him out, but in
Reuben's absence the brothers had another idea. Judah, another
son of Leah, did not realize what Reuben had in mind, and himself wanted to do something other than leave Joseph to perish
in the pit. He saw a caravan coming and, appealing to the
cupidity of the brothers, suggested that they sell Joseph. This they
did, and Joseph was carried off by the traders on their way to
Egypt. The brothers dipped Joseph's robe in blood and took it
to their father to show that Joseph must have been devoured by
a wild beast. Thus disaster struck a precocious young man.

In Act II, as we may call it, of this dramatic narrative, adversity
tests a maturing man. In Egypt Joseph was sold again, this time
to Potiphar, an officer of Pharaoh and a captain of the guard.
Here Joseph did his work so well that Potiphar made him overseer of his house. This, however, provided a great temptation,
for Potiphar's wife made advances to him and, when he repulsed
her, she "framed" him and had him imprisoned. In prison he
interpreted the dreams of two fellow prisoners, none other than

the butler and the baker of the king of Egypt, a good end being foretold for the butler, an evil end for the baker. He asked the butler to remember him, but when the latter got out he forgot all about it. Only later, when Pharaoh himself had dreams no one else could interpret, the butler remembered his imprisoned friend. Joseph was brought, gave the meaning of the dreams as portending seven good years to be followed by seven years of famine, and also proposed measures for storing food during the good years against the lean years to come. This so appealed to Pharaoh that he put Joseph in charge of what was to be done.

Joseph, now thirty years old, received from Pharaoh an Egyptian name, Zaphenath-paneah, which means "God, the living God, hath spoken," showing the strong impression Joseph had made on Pharaoh; and he married an Egyptian wife, Asenath, daughter of Potiphera, priest of On, or Heliopolis (Genesis 41:45). In the biblical text there are a number of statements about the position and responsibilities of Joseph. Comparing these with the titles found in Egyptian inscriptions, a recent study concludes that the full titulary of Joseph in a normal Egyptian arrangement was: "Overseer of the Granaries of Upper and Lower Egypt, Royal Seal-bearer, God's Father [the king is regarded as god; this title belongs to someone who, by reason of wisdom or other attribute, stands to him in the relation of a 'father'], Great Steward of the Lord of the Two Lands, Foremost of Courtiers, Chief of the Entire Land."[1]

In Act III, time turns the tables in a surprising reversal. The seven years of plenty go by. Joseph and Asenath have two sons, Manasseh and Ephraim. The seven years of famine come on. The famine extends into other lands as well. In Canaan the pinch of hunger is felt and Jacob, learning that there is grain in Egypt, sends his sons, except Benjamin, to buy grain. They must perforce present themselves before Joseph. They have no inkling of who this imposing Egyptian is, but Joseph recognizes them at once.

He devises various tests to try them, to see what kind of men they have become, to find out whether they are loyal to his father and to his younger brother. When they have come a second time and when he is satisfied that they are worthy to be forgiven, he makes himself known to them.

There are yet five years of famine to come. Joseph sends for the aged father. Jacob and his sons and daughters, and his sons' sons and his sons' daughters, all come and dwell in the land of Goshen, east of the Delta. There Israel died and thence was carried up to Canaan to be buried with Abraham and Isaac in the cave of the field at Machpelah. There in Egypt in due time, aged one hundred and ten years, Joseph died, "and they embalmed him, and he was put in a coffin in Egypt" (Genesis 50:26).

This dramatic biography embodies a daring belief, the belief that God was in control of what happened. In the whole course of events nothing obviously supernatural took place. Before and after this in the Bible we read of angels and miracles, but in the present narrative they do not appear. Everything is natural. A caravan moves across the countryside, as caravans have moved across that countryside from time immemorial until now. A famine strikes the Near East, an area of famines throughout the centuries.

But many very important things take place. The crucially important things are beyond the power of even a good man to accomplish for himself. When Joseph was down in the dry cistern, completely unable to get out, apparently doomed to die a slow and horrible death there and to have that miserable pit for his grave—a caravan came by. The fact that there is mention of a caravan of Ishmaelites from Gilead, and again of Midianite traders, may indicate that the story was told in two forms. The important matter is that such a caravan came at such a time. When Joseph was sold in Egypt, it was to an official who was willing to recognize his worth and give him a chance in his household. It might have been a different kind of man. While Joseph was in prison it came to pass that the butler and baker were cast there too and, through relationship with the butler, Joseph had a chance, however tardily, to stand before Pharaoh. The famine of course caused much suffering, but it also provided an opportunity for a man of foresight and ability. As hunger sapped their strength, the other sons looked at one another in dull bewilderment, but Jacob happened to hear that there was grain in Egypt. None of these things could Joseph have caused to take place, but they did all come to pass.

The crucially important things were also beyond the power of even bad men to keep from happening. There is no doubt that the brothers had thoroughly bad intentions. It was their intention to slay Joseph. When that intention was changed, it was still their purpose to sell him away where he would never be seen again. The chain of events, however, was such that they inevitably found themselves face to face with the very same man.

What did the things which happened accomplish? For Joseph, they led to the experience of being tested. He was tested by three major betrayals: by the envious violence of the brothers, the perverse passion of Potiphar's wife, and the casual forgetfulness of the butler. This aspect of the matter in which Joseph experienced testing is emphasized in the summary in Psalm 105:17-19: "Joseph . . . was sold as a slave. His feet were hurt with fetters, his neck was put in a collar of iron; until what he [God] had said came to pass the word of the Lord tested him." Joseph had the experience of being spared. He was on the edge of death and was delivered. Many other persons have been cast into pits and have perished there, but if one must ask why they had to die, one who has been rescued must also ask, Why have I been spared? Joseph had the experience of being sustained. He was enabled to resist when tempted, when he had to flee perhaps as much from himself as from Potiphar's wife. He was upheld with sufficient reserves during the long days in prison. He had the experience of being led. It was probably not the case that Joseph recognized at every step where he was going, but it certainly was the case that as he looked back afterward it seemed to him that he had been guided.

For the brothers other aspects of the total event came to the fore, and different results took place in their lives. They had the experience of being thwarted. They had not gotten the result they intended, namely, to be rid of that dreamer. They had gotten some results they had not intended. They poisoned all their family relationships. They started out with a crime. Then they had to deceive their father. Then they could never be sure of one another. What if one should betray the others? They had a fearful and guilty conscience. When they were in trouble in Egypt, even before they knew that the man was Joseph, they said, "In truth we are guilty concerning our brother." The whole picture of his crying to them out of the pit came again before their minds. "Therefore," they said, "is this distress come upon us" (Genesis 42:21). Even after Joseph forgave them they could not really believe it. Years later when Jacob died their first thought was that now Joseph would feel free to take his revenge on them. So the brothers were up against something bigger than themselves, something bigger than they knew they would be up against.

They also had the experience of being at least somewhat transformed. In Egypt Judah spoke for them. He was always perhaps somewhat better than the rest, yet the fact that he was their spokesman must indicate that to some extent he expressed what they thought. They brought Benjamin, the littlest one, when they came back the second time. Joseph pretended to plan to keep him as a slave. Then Judah made his plea. He spoke of the aged father's sorrow over the loss already of one son, of his fear lest something befall the youngest now, a happening which would surely bring down his gray hairs in sorrow to the grave. He, Judah, asked to be kept himself, that the littlest brother might go free. As Walter Russell Bowie comments, "Joseph's brothers had begun to learn what the real values of life are."[2]

For the event as a whole, also, the things which happened had an important result. They turned it to an unexpected, a surprising, and, to an extent beyond what one could hope for, a good outcome. Evil was actually turned into good.

What shall we call this that happened? What was it that was at work here? Was it fate? Belief in fate prevailed widely in the ancient world. The Greeks, for example, believed in the gods, but over the gods themselves was dark, inexorable fate. Some years ago Karl Heim said that fate more than any other term expresses the direction in which men are now looking for the meaning of life, and Roger Hazelton has remarked that many professing Christians are really just practicing fatalists.[3] Fate is what is decreed or spoken, therefore what cannot be taken back, what has to happen. In ordinary usage it means the impersonal, arbitrary, inevitable nature of things. Before such a nature of things, man is finally powerless, therefore his life is ultimately meaningless. Biblical faith cannot agree with fatalism because to place fate above God is to hold an unworthy view of God, and to make man a helpless victim of inscrutable necessity is to deny that his actions matter.

Was it predestination that was at work in the life of Joseph? This term means that whatever happens is God's will. Roger Hazelton remarks that predestination does not answer fatalism but simply absorbs it.[4] Applied to the story of Joseph, this would mean that it was God who made the brothers jealous and evil men, and who made it impossible for Joseph to fall when he was tempted. This too, then, gives an unworthy view of God and denies human freedom.

There is yet a third and different word by which to try to

grasp that which was at work in the whole event with which we are dealing. This is the word "providence." The word itself does not occur in the narrative, nor in fact is it found anywhere in the entire Bible except in the King James Version of Acts 24:2, where it refers to something a man has done. Nevertheless, it seems to be the best word in the English language to express an idea which runs through the entire Bible and which is the leading idea in the story of Joseph. The English word comes from two Latin words, *pro* meaning "before," and *video* (a word more familiar now than formerly) meaning "to see." The Latin *provideo* and the English "providence" therefore have as their first meaning, "to see before, to see ahead." But if you see ahead you also try to prepare for what you see, therefore the second meaning of the term is "to provide for, to care for, to look after." It is in the latter sense that the word is used in Acts 24:2 in the King James Version, where the orator Tertullus says to the governor Felix: "Seeing . . . that very worthy deeds are done unto this nation by thy providence." So if we use the word "providence" in respect to God we mean that God foresees and provides. As Georgia Harkness puts it: "To believe in divine providence is to believe that God sees the way before us and looks after us as we seek to walk in it."[5]

This, the doctrine of providence, is what our story teaches. The memorable words of Joseph in his final recorded address to his brothers in Genesis 50:20 sum it all up: "As for you, you meant evil against me; but God meant it for good." As William G. Pollard observes in discussing this very passage in his book on *Chance and Providence,* there is in Joseph's words no excusing or explaining away of the reality of responsibility, but there is also no failure to note the remarkable final outcome: "Here clearly is the certain evidence of the mighty providence of God mysteriously emerging from a long sequence of chances and accidents, working wonderfully in and through history to transform and redeem the damage and hurt wrought in the world by the evil acts of sinful men and in the end accomplishing far more than could ever have been expected or hoped for."[6]

The daring belief just described had definite benefits in the life of Joseph. The doctrine is not true because it has a beneficial effect on the person who holds it, but it is effective, we may believe, because it does correspond with how things really are. The belief in this doctrine on the part of Joseph results in humility. Joseph who says with humble recognition of the power to which he owes what has happened, "God has made me lord of all Egypt" (Genesis 45:9), is a far different man from the brash youth who boasted of his dreams of superiority. Equanimity is another result. Joseph has taken sudden reversals of fortune and staggering blows with relative steadiness. Magnanimity is also evident. In the light of all that has happened Joseph cannot think of revenge. "Fear not," he says to the brothers, "for am I in the place of God?" (Genesis 50:19). God had already taken over the situation and brought it out to a wonderful end. Why should he any longer cherish bitterness? Expectancy too resulted. Joseph must have learned that "God's hand may be moving long before it is revealed," as Walter Russell Bowie puts it.[7] Surely he could not ever again look ahead without at least some hopefulness.

It is clear that life lived in belief in the providence of God is life that is lived affirmatively. We have spoken of how Joseph was spared, sustained, and led. Referring to the same types of experience as "deliverance, buoyancy, guidance," Roger Hazelton writes:

These are not events for which we have to thank our lucky stars, but signs that the hard mold of so-called fate is cracking, that authentic light is sifting through the veil of mystery thrown up in front of God. They can only mean that a mighty Yes is spoken to us in the very midst of the nearer, louder No which seems to come from fate. And what is more, these sign-events do not represent simply the Christian believer's opinion as to what might just as easily be explained on other, utterly nonprovidential grounds. For they actually disclose and release a power to be which can only come from God. Thus human extremity gives God his opportunity, and by means of faith that opportunity becomes ours as well.[8]

NOTES

Abbreviations

ASV   American Standard Version.

BA   The Biblical Archaeologist (New Haven: The American Schools of Oriental Research).

HBD   Harper's Bible Dictionary, by Madeleine S. Miller and J. Lane Miller (New York: Harper & Brothers, 1952).

HDB   A Dictionary of the Bible, ed. by James Hastings (New York: Charles Scribner's Sons, 4 vols. 1898-1902).

IB   The Interpreter's Bible (New York and Nashville: Abingdon Press, 12 vols. 1952-57).

KJV   King James Version.

Moffatt The Old Testament, A New Translation by James Moffatt (New York: George H. Doran Company, 1924-25).

RSV   Revised Standard Version.

Chapter 1. Creation

1. Paul Tillich, *Systematic Theology* (Chicago: The University of Chicago Press), Vol. I, 1951, p. 252.

2. Langdon B. Gilkey, *Maker of Heaven and Earth* (Garden City: Doubleday, 1959), p. 260.

3. Psalm 90:2.

4. Augustine, *The City of God*, XII, 14.

5. Irenaeus, *Against Heresies*, II, x, 4.

6. *Ibid.*, III, viii, 3.

7. Cited by Walter Russell Bowie in IB 1, p. 487.

8. Irenaeus, *op. cit.*, III, viii, 3.
9. Joseph Addison, "Ode."

Chapter 2. Paradise Lost

1. Cf. HDB 1, p. 36; IB 1, p. 510.
2. HBD p. 148.
3. Carlton C. Allen, "A Voice from the Moon," in *The Reader's Digest*, May 1960, pp. 69 f.
4. In IB 1, p. 504.

Chapter 3. East of Eden, or Murder Inaugurated

1. Genesis 4:1.
2. Psalm 39:5.
3. *The Works of Lord Byron*, by J. W. Lake (Philadelphia: Grigg, Elliott & Co., 1849), p. 363 a.
4. *Ibid.*, pp. 381 b-382 a.
5. Job 15:20-24, Moffatt.
6. Sophocles, *Oedipus the King*, 463-482 (Loeb Classical Library, p. 45).
7. Genesis 4:16.
8. Genesis 4:15.
9. Alan Moorehead, *No Room in the Ark* (New York: Harper & Brothers, 1959), p. 123.
10. *Albert Schweitzer: An Anthology*, ed. by Charles R. Joy (New York: Harper & Brothers, 1947), pp. 274, 259 f.
11. In *The Christian Century*, April 6, 1960, pp. 408-409.
12. Matthew 5:21-22.
13. Walter Russell Bowie in IB 1, p. 519.

Chapter 4. The Flood

1. André Parrot, *The Flood and Noah's Ark* (New York: Philosophical Library, 1953), pp. 51-52.
2. James G. Frazer, *Folk-lore in the Old Testament; Studies in Comparative Religion, Legend and Law* (London: Macmillan and Co., Ltd., 3 vols. 1918), I, pp. 104-361.
3. Hermann Gunkel, *The Legends of Genesis* (Chicago: The Open Court Publishing Co., 1907), pp. 10-11.
4. Walter Russell Bowie in IB 1, p. 538.
5. Quoted by Parrot, *op. cit.*, pp. 70-71.

Chapter 5. Noah and His Wine

1. John Skinner, *A Critical and Exegetical Commentary on Genesis*, The International Critical Commentary (New York: Charles Scribner's Sons, 1910), p. 182.

2. S. R. Driver, *The Book of Genesis*, Westminster Commentaries (London: Methuen & Co. Ltd., 9th ed. 1913), pp. 108-109.

3. Ruth Dye.

4. Dr. Richard C. Cabot, quoted in *The Christian Case for Abstinence* (New York: Association Press, 1955), p. 188.

5. Emil Bogen, M.D., and Lehmann W. S. Hisey, *What About Alcohol?* (Los Angeles: published by Angelus Press for the Scientific Education Association, 1946), p. 65.

6. Quoted in Upton Sinclair, *The Cup of Fury* (Great Neck, N.Y.: Channel Press, 1956), p. 49.

7. Quoted *ibid.*, pp. 53-54.

8. Cuthbert A. Simpson in IB 1, p. 556.

9. Quoted in Upton Sinclair, *The Cup of Fury*, pp. 19-22.

10. Driver, *The Book of Genesis*, p. 109.

11. Skinner, *A Critical and Exegetical Commentary on Genesis*, p. 185.

12. James A. Pike, *Beyond Anxiety* (New York: Charles Scribner's Sons, 1953), pp. 52-53.

13. Sinclair, *The Cup of Fury*, p. 12.

14. *Ibid.*, pp. 175-176.

15. *What About Alcohol?* by Emil Bogen, M.D., and Lehmann W. S. Hisey, Preface by Haven Emerson, M.D. (Los Angeles: published by Angelus Press for the Scientific Education Association, 1946), pp. 79-82.

Chapter 6. The Family of Man

1. John Skinner, *A Critical and Exegetical Commentary on Genesis* (The International Critical Commentary), p. 189.

2. Strabo, *Geography*, XVI, iv, 8.

3. Edwin G. Conklin, *The Direction of Human Evolution* (New York: Charles Scribner's Sons, 1921), p. 34. Quoted in Robert E. Speer, *Of One Blood* (New York: Council of Women for Home Missions and Missionary Education Movement of the United States and Canada, 1924), p. 22.

4. *Papers on Interracial Problems, Presented to the First Universal Races Congress, Held at the University of London, July 26-29, 1911,* ed. by G. Spiller (London: King and Son, 1911), p. 21. Quoted by Speer, *ibid.*

5. Benjamin E. Mays, *Seeking to be Christian in Race Relations* (New York: Friendship Press, 1957), p. 10.

6. *The Family of Man, The Photographic Exhibition Created by Edward Steichen for the Museum of Modern Art* (published for the Museum of Modern Art by Simon and Schuster, 1955).

Chapter 7. The Tower of Babel

1. W. F. Albright, *From the Stone Age to Christianity* (Baltimore: The Johns Hopkins Press, 2d ed. 1946), p. 6.
2. André Parrot, *Babylon and the Old Testament* (New York: Philosophical Library, 1958), pp. 15-16.
3. André Parrot, *The Tower of Babel* (New York: Philosophical Library, 1955), p. 26.
4. Reinhold Niebuhr, *Beyond Tragedy* (New York: Charles Scribner's Sons, 1937), p. 38.
5. Pitirim A. Sorokin, *The Crisis of Our Age* (New York: E. P. Dutton and Co., Inc., 1943), p. 303.
6. Quoted by Reinhold Niebuhr, *Beyond Tragedy*, p. 37.
7. Walter Russell Bowie in IB 1, pp. 562-563.

Chapter 8. Abraham: Man of Faith

1. Julius Wellhausen, *Prolegomena to the History of Israel* (Edinburgh: Adam & Charles Black, 1885), pp. 318-319.
2. *Ibid.*, p. 320.
3. Nelson Glueck, *Rivers in the Desert, A History of the Negev* (New York: Farrar, Straus and Cudahy, 1959), pp. 68-69.
4. Nelson Glueck in *The Holy Land, New Light on the Prehistory and Early History of Israel*, published in co-operation with the Hebrew University, Department of Antiquities, Israel Exploration Society, *Antiquity and Survival* Vol. II:2-3 (The Hague: N.V. Electrische Drukkerij en Uitgeverij "Luctor et Emergo," 1957), p. 275.
5. Y. Aharoni, "The Land of Gerar," a paper published in Hebrew in *Eretz-Israel* 3 (1954), pp. 108-111, and in English in *Israel Exploration Journal* 6 (1956), pp. 26-32, see especially p. 31.
6. Nelson Glueck, *Rivers in the Desert*, p. 31.
7. Friedrich Cornelius, "Genesis XIV," in *Zeitschrift für die alttestamentliche Wissenschaft* 72 (1960), pp. 1-7; and for the date of Hammurabi see F. Cornelius, "Chronology. Eine Erwiderung," in *Journal of Cuneiform Studies* 12 (1958), pp. 101-104.
8. John Bright, *A History of Israel* (Philadelphia: The Westminster Press, 1959), p. 63.
9. *Ibid.*, p. 67.
10. Julius Wellhausen, *Reste arabischen Heidentums gesammelt und erläutert*, 2d ed. (Berlin: G. Reimer, 1897).
11. George E. Mendenhall, "Covenant Forms in Israelite Tradition," in BA 17 (1954), pp. 53-54.
12. Albrecht Alt, *Der Gott der Väter*, Beiträge zur Wissenschaft

vom Alten und Neuen Testament, 48 (Stuttgart: W. Kohlhammer Verlag, 1929), p. 73.

13. W. F. Albright, *From the Stone Age to Christianity* (Baltimore: The Johns Hopkins Press, 2d ed. 1946), p. 189.

14. Mendenhall, *op. cit.*, p. 62.

Chapter 9. Sodom and Gomorrah: Can It Happen Now?

1. T. K. Cheyne in *New World* (Boston), June 1892, cited by S. R. Driver, *The Book of Genesis* (London: Methuen & Co. Ltd., 9th ed. 1913), p. 203. See also T. K. Cheyne, "Sodom and Gomorrah," in *Encyclopaedia Biblica* (New York: The Macmillan Company), 4 (1903), cols. 4666-4679, especially col. 4670.

2. Hermann Gunkel, *Genesis,* Handkommentar zum Alten Testament (Göttingen: Vandenhoeck and Ruprecht, 1st ed. 1901), 3d ed. 1910, pp. 214-217.

3. Driver, *The Book of Genesis,* p. 203.

4. *Ibid.,* p. 191.

5. George Adam Smith in *Encyclopaedia Biblica* 1 (1899), col. 552.

6. A. P. Stanley, *Sinai and Palestine in Connexion with their History* (1864), quoted by Driver, *The Book of Genesis,* p. 152; HDB 3, p. 150.

7. Emil G. Kraeling, *Rand McNally Bible Atlas* (Chicago: Rand McNally & Company, 1956), p. 65.

8. Lane, quoted by Driver, *The Book of Genesis,* p. 192.

9. Jerome, *Epistle* 108.

10. Josephus, *Antiquities* I, 203 (= I, xi, 4).

11. *Idem.*

12. D. H. Kallner-Amiran, "A Revised Earthquake-Catalogue of Palestine," in *Israel Exploration Journal* 1 (1950-1951), pp. 223-246; 2 (1952), pp. 48-65, and see especially p. 57.

13. Friedrich Cornelius in *Zeitschrift für die alttestamentliche Wissenschaft* 72 (1960), pp. 5-6.

14. Josephus, *The Jewish War* IV, 479 (= IV, viii, 4).

15. Friedrich Cornelius in *op. cit.*, p. 6.

16. Nelson Glueck as quoted in *Christianity Today,* July 18, 1960, p. 28.

Chapter 10. The Sacrifice (Almost) of Isaac

1. S. R. Driver, *The Book of Genesis,* p. 216.

2. John Skinner, *A Critical and Exegetical Commentary on Genesis,* p. 328.

3. Nelson Glueck, *Rivers in the Desert, A History of the Negev* (New York: Farrar, Straus and Cudahy, 1959), p. 61.

4. Quoted by J. J. S. Perowne in *The Great Texts of the Bible,* ed. by James Hastings, *Genesis to Numbers* (New York: Charles Scribner's Sons, 1911), pp. 193-194.

5. F. W. Robertson in *The Great Texts of the Bible, Genesis to Numbers,* p. 195.

6. *The Second Shepherds' Play, Everyman, and Other Early Plays,* translated by Clarence G. Child, The Riverside Literature Series (Boston: Houghton Mifflin Company, 1910), pp. 14-16.

7. Walter Russell Bowie in IB 1, p. 643.

Chapter 11. Climbing Jacob's Ladder with Him

1. George Arthur Buttrick, *Sermons Preached in a University Church* (New York and Nashville: Abingdon Press, 1959), pp. 13-19.

2. Walter Russell Bowie in IB 1, pp. 691-692.

Chapter 12. The Providence of God in Joseph's Life and Ours

1. W. A. Ward, "The Egyptian Office of Joseph," in *Journal of Semitic Studies* 5 (1960), pp. 144-150, see especially p. 150.

2. Walter Russell Bowie in IB 1, p. 796.

3. Roger Hazelton, *God's Way with Man* (New York and Nashville: Abingdon Press, 1956), pp. 34-35.

4. *Ibid.,* p. 59.

5. Georgia Harkness, *The Providence of God* (New York and Nashville: Abingdon Press, 1960), p. 17.

6. William G. Pollard, *Chance and Providence* (New York: Charles Scribner's Sons, 1958), p. 132.

7. Walter Russell Bowie in IB 1, p. 800.

8. Roger Hazelton, *God's Way with Man,* p. 57.

Indexes

NAME AND SUBJECT INDEX

Abamram, 91
A-bar-gi, 113
Abel, 27-28, 30-31, 33-34, 38, 45-46
Abimelech, 89-90
Abiram, 114
Abraham, 85-99, 100-104, 106, 110,
    112-123, 125, 131, 136
Abram, 85, 91
Adam, 19-20, 24, 27-29, 34, 45,
    48, 86, 95
Addison, Joseph, 17
Admah, 102, 104, 107, 109
Africa, 34-35, 40, 66
Aharoni, Y., 90
Ahura Mazda, 15
Ai, 101
Air Line Pilots Association, 53
Akkadian language, 42
Akkadians, 77
Alalakh, 108
Albright, W. F., 76
Alcoholics Anonymous, 63
Allen, Carlton C., 22
Alt, Albrecht, 96
America, 40, 76, 119
Amorite, 65
Amraphel, 93
Anderson, Sherwood, 62

Andrews, C. F., 72
animism, 94
anthropology, 27
Apollodorus, 41
Arabia, 21, 33, 66-67, 100
Aram, 65, 67, 94, 105
Ararat, 43, 48, 51-54
Arioch, 93
Armenia, 52, 54
Arpachshad, 65, 85
Asenath, 135
Asher, 132
Ashurbanipal, 42
Asia, 40
Asia Minor, 66-67
Asians, 92
Asshur, 65, 67
Assyria, 20-21, 67
Atlantic, 52, 66
Augustine, 12, 121
Australia, 40

Babel, 74-85
Bab-ilani, 77
Bab-ilu, 77
Babylon, 42, 75-79, 91
Babylonia, 67, 93
Babylonians, 11, 42, 45

151

Bahrein, 74-75
Baney, Ralph E., 109
baptism, 49
Barnabas, Epistle of, 121
Beer-sheba, 90, 107, 114, 125
Beitin, 125
Bela, 102
Beni Hasan, 92
Beni Nacim, 104
Benjamin, 132, 135, 138
Bennett, John C., 36
Berriault, Gina, 110
Bethel, 88, 101, 114, 125, 127
Bethlehem, 104, 132
Bethuel, 122
Bilhah, 132
Blumenbach, Johann Friedrich, 67
Boghazköy, 92-93
Borneo, 40
Bowie, Walter Russell, 38, 47, 83,
    121, 129, 139, 141
Boyd, Bud, 79-80
Brahmanas, 41
Bright, John, 94
British Museum, 42
Brooke, Rupert, 126
Brunner, Emil, 24
Burj Beitin, 101
Burma, 40
Buttrick, George Arthur, 126
Byblus, 113
Byron, 29, 31

Cabot, Richard C., 55
Caesarea, 109
Cain, 27-38, 46, 54
Cairo, 92
Canaan, 64-67, 87, 97, 101-102,
    112-114, 122, 124, 130, 132, 135-
    136
Canaanites, 66, 133
Caphar-barucha, 104
Caphtorim, 65
Caspian Sea, 66
catacombs, 121
Caucasian, 67-68
Chagar Bazar, 91

Chaldeans, 88
Charing Cross, 126
Cheyne, T. K., 100
China, 40, 76
Chedorlaomer, 93
Chile, 39
church, 49
circumcision, 96-97
Conklin, Edwin G., 68
Convent of Saint Catherine, 48
Cook, George Cram, 62
Copernicus, 9
covenant, 94-97
Columbus, 119
Crane, Stephen, 62
creation, 9-18
Crete, 108
Cush, 21, 64-66

Dan, 132
Darwin, 9
Dead Sea, 93, 102, 104-109
Debs, Eugene V., 56, 62
Dedan, 67
Delta, 136
Deukalion, 41
Dilmun, 74-75
Dooley, Thomas, 68
Dothan, 134
Driver, S. R., 59, 81, 100-101, 112
dualism, 13-15, 23, 25
Duncan, Isadora, 62
Dunne, Finley Peter, 62

Ea, 41-42
Eber, 85
Eden, 20-27, 29, 33, 39, 102
E document, 87
Egypt, 15, 21, 41, 64-66, 76, 79, 81,
    92-93, 102, 113, 134-138
Egyptians, 11
Eisenhower, Dwight D., 71
el, 93, 95
Elam, 65, 67, 93
Elath, 106
El-Elohe-Israel, 130
Eliezer, 91

Ellasar, 93
El Shaddai, 96
Emerson, Haven, 63
Engedi, 104
Enlil, 43
Enoch, 45-46, 95, 97
Enosh, 45
Ephraim, 135
Ephron, 92
Esau, 122-124, 129-130, 132
E-temen-an-ki, 79
Ethiopia, 21, 66, 81
Ethiopians, 21
Euphrates, 20-21, 40, 75-76, 79, 95
Eusebius, 113
Eve, 27, 29
Execration Texts, 92

fatalism, 139
Fear of Isaac, 96
Federal Aviation Agency, 53
Felix, 140
Fertile Crescent, 75-76, 92
Flood, 39-51, 85
Fort, Joel, 62
Frazer, James G., 40

Gad, 132
Galilee, Sea of, 102
Gandhi, Mahatma, 72
Ganges, 21
Gaza, 90
Geneva, 81
Gentiles, 99
ger, 89
Gerar, 89-90
Gibson, Althea, 71
Gihon, 20-21
Gilead, 136
Gilkey, Langdon, 12
Girgashite, 65
Glueck, Nelson, 89-90, 94, 109, 114, 117
Goiim, 93
Gomer, 64
Gomorrah, 100-111
Goshen, 136

Göttingen University, 67
Greece, 40-41, 100
Greeks, 11, 16, 139
Green, Jack D., 37
Gunkel, Hermann, 44, 47, 100

Hagar, 91, 95, 112
Ham, 48, 59, 64, 66, 85
Hammurabi, 93
Haran, 88, 91, 95, 97, 101, 122, 127
Harkness, Georgia, 140
Hastings, James, 113
Hattusa, 93
Havilah, 21
Hazelton, Roger, 139, 141
Hebrew University, Jerusalem, 107
Hebron, 92, 103-104, 125, 134
Heim, Karl, 139
Heliopolis, 135
henotheism, 96
Henry, O., 62
Herod the Great, 103
Herodotus, 79
Heth, 67
Hiddekel, 20-21
Hiel, 114
Hit, 77
Hittites, 67, 91-93, 124
Hoover, J. Edgar, 33
Howard University, 71
Huleh, Lake, 102
Hurrites, 93

Ibsha, 92
India, 21, 34, 40-41, 65, 76
Indianapolis Church Federation, 73
Indo-Europeans, 66, 85
Indus, 21, 76
Industrial Workers of the World, 56
Ionian Greeks, 66
Iran, 74
Irenaeus, 13-14, 17, 121
Isaac, 85-87, 95-97, 112-122, 125, 130-132, 136
Iscah, 122
Ishmael, 91, 95, 112
Ishmaelites, 136

Israel, 86, 95-96, 118, 131, 136
Israelites, 11, 17, 43, 45-46, 85-86
Issachar, 132

Jabbok, 129
Jacob, 85-87, 91, 95-97, 122-132,
    135-136, 138
Japan, 34, 39-40
Japheth, 48, 59, 64, 66, 85
Jared, 45
Javan, 64, 66
J document, 87
Jebel Sudum, 105
Jebusites, 65, 67
Jephthah, 114
Jericho, 75, 101, 106, 114
Jerome, 104
Jerusalem, 67, 101, 103, 105, 107,
    114, 125
Jesus Christ, 30, 38, 121
Jews, 99
Jewish New Year Festival, 118
Johnson, Mordecai, 71
Jordan, 101-102, 105, 107
Joseph, 131-142
Josephus, 21, 105-106
Jubal, 46
Judah, 131, 134, 138-139
Judah, region, 88
Judea, 101

Ka-dingir, 77
Kallner-Amiran, D. H., 107
Kansas City, Missouri, 109
Kenan, 45
Kephar Barikha, 104
Khalil, el-, 98
kikkar, 101
King List, 45
Kish, 40
Kittim, 65
Koldewey, Robert, 79
Kraeling, Emil G., 102
Kudur-Lagamara, 93

Laban, 122, 127-128
Lamech, 33, 36, 45-46, 49, 56

Lawson, James M., Jr., 69
League of Fighting Godless, 81
League of Nations, 81
Leah, 127-128, 131-132, 134
legend, 44, 86, 88, 100
Leiser, Bill, 72
Levi, 131
Lewis, Sinclair, 62
Little Rock, Arkansas, 70-71
Liverpool, 126
London, 126
London, Jack, 57, 61-62
Lot, 89, 93, 101-106, 109-110, 122
Lud, 65
Ludim, 65
Luschan, von, 68
Luxor, 92
Luz, 125

Machpelah, 92, 136
Madai, 64, 66
Magog, 64
Mahalalel, 45
Malaya, 40
Mamre, 103
Manasseh, 114, 135
Manu, 41
Mari, 91-93, 122
Mays, Benjamin E., 68
Medes, 66
Media, 66
Mediterranean, 66, 108
Megiddo, 114
Mes-Anne-Pada, 78
Mesha, 114
Meshech, 64
Mesopotamia, 20-21, 39-41, 43, 74-
    79, 88, 91-93, 113, 122, 124
Methuselah, 45, 49
midbar, 134
Midianites, 136
Mighty One of Jacob, 96
Milcah, 122
Millay, Edna St. Vincent, 62
Mitchell, James P., 71
Mizraim, 66
Moab, 101, 106, 114

Mohenjo-daro, 76
Molech, 118
Mongolian, 67
monism, 14-15, 23, 25
Moorehead, Alan, 34
Moriah, 117
Moses, 96
Mount Sodom, 105
Muhammad, 94
Museum of Modern Art, 69
myth, 7, 11, 44, 86, 100

Nabonidus, 78
Nabopolassar, 79
Nahor, 85, 91, 95, 122
Nakhur, 91, 122
Naphtali, 132
narcotic, 55
naturalism, 24-25
Nazirite, 62
Nebuchadnezzar, 75, 79
Negeb, 88-90, 114
Negroid, 68
New York City, 53, 126
Niebuhr, Reinhold, 81
Nile, 21, 66, 102, 113
Nimrod, 65
Nineveh, 40, 42
Nippur, 42
Nisir, 42
Noah, 34, 43, 45, 47-49, 51-59, 64-65, 85-86, 95
Nod, 33
Nubia, 66
Nuzi, 91, 128

Oakland, California, 57
On, 135
Ophir, 21, 65
Oppert, Jules, 45

Pacific, 39-40
Paddan-aram, 127, 132
Palestine, 20-21, 40, 43, 52, 65-66, 75, 88-89, 92-93, 101-102, 107, 109, 125, 134
Palmer, Alice Freeman, 16

Palmer, George Herbert, 16
pantheism, 14
paradise, 19-26, 29, 46
Parnassus, Mount, 41
Parrot, André, 40, 78
patriarchs, 85-88, 92, 94
Paul, 98, 109, 121
Paula, 104
P document, 87
Peleg, 85
Persia, 15
Persian Gulf, 40, 67, 74
Pharaoh, 134-136
Philae, 113
Philistines, 89-90
Philo, 115
philosophy, 10-11
Phoenicians, 66, 113
Pike, James A., 60
Pishon, 20-21
Pliny, 21
Pollard, William G., 140
polydaemonism, 94
Polynesia, 40
polytheism, 95
Pontus, 54
Potiphar, 134, 137
Potiphera, 135
predestination, 139
Procopius, 113
providence, 140-141
provideo, 140
Put, 64
Pyrrha, 41

Queen Mary (ship), 48, 55

Rachel, 127-128, 132
Ramet el-Khalil, 103
Re, 15
Rebekah, 122, 124, 132
Red Sea, 67
Reu, 85
Reuben, 131, 134
Rickey, Branch, 72
Robertson, F. W., 118
Robinson, Edward, 117

Robinson, Jackie, 72
Romans, 16
Rome, 52, 121
Russell, Leah, 71

Sacy, le Maistre de, 49
Salt Sea, 105, 108
San Francisco, 53
San Francisco Bay, 34
San Quentin Prison, 37
Sarah, 104, 112, 115, 119
Sarai, 91
Schweitzer, Albert, 35
science, 9-11
Seabrook, William, 62
Seba, 21, 66
Senate Interstate Commerce Com-
    mittee, 53
Septuagint, 87, 116
Serug, 85
Seth, 45, 95
sexagesimal system, 45
Shakespeare, 119
Shang, Great City, 76
Shargalisharri, 77
Sheba, 21, 67
Shechem, 88, 130, 134
Shelah, 85
Shem, 48, 59, 64-65, 67, 85
Sheng, Sing, 70
Shinar, 74-75, 93
shophar, 119
Shub-ad, 113
Shulgi, 78
Shuruppak, 40
Siddim, 105, 108
Sidon, 65, 67
Simeon, 131
Simpson, Cuthbert A., 24, 58
Sinai, 48, 115, 117
Sinclair, Upton, 58-59, 61
Skinner, John, 54, 65, 81, 112
Smith, George, 42, 101
Sodom, 100-111
Solomon, 117
Sorokin, Pitirim A., 81-82
Spain, 65-66

Stakhanov movement, 82
Steichen, Edward, 69
Sterling, George, 62
Strabo, 67
Sumatra, 40
Sumerians, 41-42, 45-46, 74-77, 95
Syria, 67, 75, 108

Tarshish, 65-66
tell, 134
Tell Abu Hureira, 90
Tell Abu Matar, 114
Terah, 85, 95, 97
Tertullus, 140
theology, 11
Thomas, Dylan, 62
Thompson, Francis, 126
Tidal, 93
Tigris, 21, 40, 75
Tillich, Paul, 10
time, 12, 15-16
Tiras, 64
Tokyo, 37
Traubel, Helen, 127
Tubal, 64
Tubal-cain, 36, 46
Tudhaliyas, 93

Ugarit, 108
United Nations, 37, 110
United States of America, 34, 36,
    52, 56, 62, 110
United States Supreme Court, 70
University Museum of the Univer-
    sity of Pennsylvania, 42
Ur, Ur of the Chaldees, 40, 76, 78,
    88, 95, 97, 113
Ur-Nammu, 78
Uruk, 40
Ussher, James, 87
U.S.S.R., 36

Vanderbilt   University   Divinity
    School, 69
Vedas, 41

Wadi esh-Shari'ah, 90

Washington, 110
Wellhausen, 86-87, 94
Woolley, C. Leonard, 113
World War I, 47
World War II, 47

Ya'qob-el, 91

Zaphenath-paneah, 135

Zeboiim, 102, 104, 107, 109
Zebulun, 132
Zeus, 40
ziggurat, 78
Zillah, 31
Zilpah, 132
Zoar, 102, 104-106
Zoor, 106, 109
Zughar, 106

Scripture Index

GENESIS

Reference	Page
1:1	12
1:1-2:3	9-18
1:2	13
2:4-3:24	19
2:7	19, 20
2:8	20, 22
2:15	24
2:19	20
3:17	20
3:19	24
3:22	24
4	27-38
4:2	54
4:15	33
4:16	33
4:25	20
4:26	95
5:1	20
5:1-9:17	39-50
5:22	95
5:27	49
5:29	56
6:5	46
6:12	46
8:21	43
9:1-17	46
9:8 f.	95
9:18-29	51-63
9:20	54
9:24	58
10	64-73
10:7	21
10:29	21
11	122
11:1-9	74-84
11:2	74-76
11:3	77
11:4	77, 81, 82
11:5	83
11:9	77, 83
11:10	85
11:10-17:27	85-99
11:31	88
12	101
12:4	87
12:6	88
12:7	95
12:8	88
12:9	89
12:10	89
13	101, 105
13:1, 3	89
13:2, 5	90
13:12	89
13:18	103
14	93, 100, 102, 105, 107
14:3	108
14:12	102
14:22	95
15	96, 98
15:1	95
15:4	91
15:6	97
17	97-98
17:1	95-97
18-19	103, 107, 100-111
18:1	95
19	109
19:1	103
19:9	103
19:16	111
19:24-25	106
19:25	107
19:28	106
19:30	110
20-23	112-121
20:1	89
21:6	112

21:32 89
21:33 ....95, 114
22 112
22:1 95,
           116-117
22:2 115
22:19 114
23:9 92
23:11 92
23:17 92
24:36 122-130
24:3 95
24:62 89
25:34 124
26:1, 8 89
26:24 95
28:12 127
28:13 95-96
28:15 125
29:17 133
29:20 127
31:42 96
35:22-26 131
37-50 131-142
37:2 133
37:3 132
37:4 133
37:5 133
39:6 133
41:45 135
42:21 138
45:9 141
49:24 95
50:19 141
50:20 140
50:26 136

EXODUS
3:15 96

LEVITICUS
18:21 118
26:31 43

NUMBERS
6 62
11:7 21

DEUTERONOMY
29:23 107
33:27 126

JOSHUA
24:2 .... 43, 95

JUDGES
11:30 114
19 109

II SAMUEL
13:18 133

I KINGS
14 109
16:34 114

II KINGS
3:27 114
16:3 114
21:6 114

II CHRONICLES
3:1 117

JOB
15:20-24 32

PSALMS
19 17
39:5 27
90:2 12
105:17-19 137

PROVERBS
23:31 54

ISAIAH
15:5 106

JEREMIAH
19:5 118
48:4 106

EZEKIEL
16:46 105
20:31 118

DANIEL
11:2 75

HOSEA
11:8 107

MATTHEW
5:21-22 38

ACTS
7:8 86
24:2 140

ROMANS
1 109
4:11 99
4:12 98
8:32 121

I TIMOTHY
5:23 60

HEBREWS
7:4 86
11:4 28
11:7 117
11:8-10 97
11:17-18 115
13:2 110

JAMES
1:13 116-117
2:21 115
2:23 98

I PETER
3:20 49

II PETER
1:16 7
2:7 110
2:9 111